Health and Blessings

M Ol

The Eyes Don't See What the Mind Don't Know

A Physician's Journey to Faith

146079

The Eyes Don't See What the Mind Don't Know

A Physician's Journey to Faith

By Mike Litrel, M.D.
Edited by Ann Litrel

WRITERS ROOM BOOKS
Doylestown, Pennsylvania
2004

Dedicated to my mentor, James Cross, M.D.,
a real doctor, a real human being.

And in memory of Tammy Kay Reece,
a mother always in my thoughts.

Profits from the sale of this book will be donated to charity.

Table of Contents

Preface

I was going through some old files one day when I redis-
covered a story written by a writer who was a professed Christian. The piece had its merits, but the writing struck me as
the work of a self-centered soul in need of some growing up.
I would learn little from him. Normally I would have shelved
the article in favor of something more enlightening. But the
story left me feeling quite disturbed—the writer was me.

Thirty years ago, as a boy with dreams of becoming a
doctor, I imagined that practicing medicine might be a bit
like living inside an action movie, always knowing how to
help someone, doing it, and maybe feeling like a hero. I have
found instead that the role of doctor is more supporting actor
than main character. It is God who is the true Physician, the

source of all healing. I simply play my part and help Him as best I can.

I became an obstetrician and gynecologist because I wanted to specialize in health care for women. I studied eight years at Emory University in Atlanta—four in medical school and four in postgraduate training—and have spent almost a decade now in private practice. After all that time, I still can imagine nothing more rewarding than caring for women. From the moment I delivered my first baby as a third-year medical student, I have been captivated and awed by the process of childbirth. Women's bodies are vessels for life: caring for them is a chance to participate in the dance of Creation each and every day.

Over the years, my patients have given me more than I can ever hope to repay. They have freely poured out their trust and love, and in so doing, they have opened for me, their physician, a window into the ongoing miracle of God's work. In relating their experiences in these pages, I hope to share with you what they have taught me. All of these tales were previously published, and all are true. I have changed names and details to preserve privacy. If you think you recognize someone in this book, it is merely a coincidence. But if you recognize yourself, it is no coincidence at all, for we are all God's children, united by a bloodline of common feelings, joys, and sorrows.

I'm a believer in the adage that says, "we teach best

that which we most need to learn." I have written with an open heart about who I have been and am, seeking to honor the honesty with which my patients have shared their stories with me. The result is sometimes a picture of myself that is unflattering. If I give offense, please forgive me—God is still teaching me my part.

Introduction

    As I was bringing together the elements of this book, I encountered a patient whose story not only seemed to sum up my theme, but also inspired the title.

    As usual with my patients, I was visiting with her in the hour before her surgery. We reviewed her history and I answered her last-minute questions and concerns. Being operated on can be frightening. The time I spend with a patient in conversation during those final minutes helps reassure her about the journey we are about to take together into the operating room. Finally, when all the questions have been answered, we come to the most important part. With the patient's permission, we pray—sometimes aloud, sometimes in silence. I always ask for God's guidance for me and healing for her.

My patients are usually generous with their permissions. Many count themselves among the faithful of some flock or other. But even those who aren't are genuinely respectful of the beliefs of others. None of my patients has ever objected to a prayer, and all seem grateful—all except one.

Elizabeth came to me complaining of severe pelvic pain. We found a cystic tumor on her right ovary. An ultrasound picture suggested that her mass was not cancer, but it was large. I decided to order a CAT scan to take a better look.

The scan confirmed my initial diagnosis, but it also revealed a second tumor, hidden in her left kidney. I consulted a urological surgeon who suspected cancer and recommended surgery. The plan was for me to remove the ovarian mass at the same time.

There are few life events as chilling as uncovering cancer. It's like finding a traitor in your own body. The specter of death strikes terror in even the most faithful among us. At times like these, you rely utterly on your physician to tell you the truth, guide you toward the right medical decisions and treatment, but also to paint a picture of hope.

Elizabeth was no exception. She was frightened—panicked—by the prospect of surgery. Her eyes filled with tears when she spoke of her two children—a boy of six and a two-year-old daughter. But she attacked her diagnosis with the discipline of the scientist she was. Elizabeth was a graduate of Georgia Tech with a major in computer programming. She researched her cancer relentlessly on the Internet, appearing at appointments leading up to her surgery armed with a new batch of statistics and an organized list of questions. In this battle with fear, her weapon of choice was her formidable intellect. She wanted to know exactly what was happening to her—and, most critically, her chances of survival.

The day of her surgery finally arrived. We met in the holding room and discussed her last minute concerns. And then I asked her if it was okay for me to say a prayer. Her answer was abrupt.

"I'm not very comfortable with that," she told me, somewhat agitated. "If I'd known you were like *that*, I might not have even had you as my surgeon."

This set me back on my heels. The last thing a doctor wants to do is upset a patient as she's being wheeled into surgery. I reassured her that my medical and surgical training had been rigorous and fully accredited. She would have the advantage of the latest clinically documented research and knowledge in the field of gynecological surgery. My efforts seemed to work as the furrows in her forehead smoothed out and the anesthesia team wheeled her to the operating room.

Despite my experiences to the contrary, I know that Elizabeth is not alone in her rejection of the Divine. To some people, the idea of relying on a Supreme Being is more unsettling than relying on nothing at all. Such reliance seems illogical. It places you in the realm of the Unseen; it makes you answerable to an all powerful Being. To the scientifically minded, the physical world of the five senses is a more comfortable place, where things are neither more nor less than they appear to be. Yes, you may still be vulnerable to life's uncertainties, but when you view yourself and everything around you as an accident of nature, at least you don't have to claim ultimate responsibility.

In the end, for both the casually religious and the unbelieving, it's easier to just keep the eyes focused on the veneer of everyday life, and avoid inspecting what's going on beneath the surface.

During the course of Elizabeth's treatment, I often recalled a quotation I first heard in my surgical training—*the eyes don't see what the mind don't know*. The saying was used then to describe the discoveries of Dr. William Saye and the late Dr. Cullen Richardson, two leading physicians who revolutionized the field of pelvic reconstructive surgery. For me, "The eyes don't see what the mind don't know" came to describe much more than my feelings about surgery itself—it summed up the relationship between spiritual and physical health.

Surgery is the field of medicine that tackles problems of the body which are physically apparent: tumors, hernias, broken bones—problems we can see and fix. But not all anatomical structures are equally visible. Dr. Richardson's contribution to pelvic reconstructive surgery was to better define the complex anatomical problems that arise from a woman giving birth. These include the breakdown of the structural supports of the bladder, uterus, and intestines. Dr. Saye's contribution was to develop laparoscopic surgical techniques to precisely view and fix these problems.

A surgeon who attended the joint lecture they gave on their research was so impressed by their innovation that he was moved to coin a way of explaining the new approach in plain English: "The eyes don't see what the mind don't know." The saying caught on. Thousands of surgeons had not been able to see the anatomical defects that were right before their eyes until Dr. Richardson explained them. Only then could Dr. Saye shine the light of the laparoscopic camera inside and determine precisely how to fix the problem with minimal trauma. What Dr. Richardson had explained, Dr. Saye could demonstrate and repair.

"The eyes don't see what the mind don't know." It's as simple as that. If you don't know what you are looking for, you are not going to find it. Faith in God is like an extra sense. If you do not have it, like my dear patient Elizabeth, you overlook the underlying anatomy of your life. You cannot see the miracles, the gifts, the purpose of your life and its obstacles, even when they are right in front of you.

So many of our problems are spiritual rather than biological. When we view our lives through the eyes of faith, the problems become clear. We are not human beings having spiritual problems—we are spiritual beings having human problems.

Six months after her surgery, Elizabeth came in for her final postoperative appointment. She was well healed and free from pain. The pelvic mass I removed which had caused her so much suffering was not cancerous. The mass on her kidney, however, was. But it had not had time to spread, and with its removal she was cured once and for all. The kidney cancer had been small, and had it not been for the ovarian tumor, it would have escaped notice until it was too late.

Faith tells me that this discovery was more than chance. I think about Elizabeth with profound gratitude for the pain caused by her benign tumor. It saved her life. Before she left me for the last time to enjoy her renewed good health, I decided to risk offending her again. I expressed my belief that God had helped us save her life, for her sake and for mine, and most importantly, for her two children.

She smiled, and her reply was a small miracle of its own. "I've kind of been thinking about that myself."

This book is about the lessons God has sent me, on life, purpose, joy, and pain. The lessons are all from my patients' stories, seen through the eyes of faith.

It Hurts to Be Here

— Rock Bottom —

— The Correct Dose —

— A Broken Heart —

— A "Celestial Discharge" —

*"Pain is the breaking of the shell
that encloses our understanding."*
–Kahlil Gibran

"Jesus wept."
John 11:35

It hurts to be born. We enter this world, each of us, in a crushing explosion of blood and fear and suffocation. Our birth is greeted with tears of pain and tears of joy from those who were expecting our arrival.

We cry. And we continue our journey of growth. In the blink of an eye we grow into toddlers. We stumble around and bump our heads. We cry some more. We become children. We await life's magical moments—Santa's arrival, our first lost tooth. We learn to follow our parents' rules. We become adolescents, agonizing, waiting for cars and freedom. We hunger for our friends' approval, yearn for our first kiss. We are grownups, confronting responsibilities and fears we had never imagined. And then, perhaps, we have children of our own, and grandchildren. And we cry some more.

Finally we die, and we are mourned by those we leave

behind.

From the moment we leave our mothers' bodies we suffer. This is the experience of being human.

Jesus suffered. His suffering and his humanity had purpose, for his death led to the transformation of mankind, freeing us of our inherent sin. God has purpose in our suffering, too—through it He enters our lives, and transforms our understanding, teaching us best what we most need to learn. How clearly we grasp His purpose, and what we make of His lessons, depends entirely upon our faith.

The stories that follow illustrate how some of our fellow human beings have made something out of their suffering. They rose above their pain, and in their transformation, they approached the Divine.

Rock Bottom

Like the stock market, my days in residency training in Atlanta's Grady Hospital were a string of ups and downs—some ups, but many more downs. At Grady it was usually a bear market. Medicine and surgery supplied the highs, but the suffering of the patients at Grady sometimes imparted the feeling of a crash.

Grady Hospital has always been the last refuge of Atlanta's sickest and poorest residents. It was founded in 1892 as a charity hospital, with 110 beds—ten for paying patients, 100 for charity. In the span of a century it has grown into the mammoth institution it is today, serving over 750,000 patients a year. The bulk of its never-ending work is ground out, day after day, by the physicians in the residency programs of

Atlanta's great medical school, the School of Medicine at Emory University. The school's young resident physicians are baptized each year in the torrential flood of the indigent, the drug addicted, the abused, and the homeless.

Like every other resident, I was baptized, too. I'll never forget a homeless cocaine addict who had been in the hospital six weeks when I met her. Beaten and raped by multiple attackers, she'd been found half buried in a parking lot behind a crack house. Thinking she was dead, her attackers had tried to conceal her body. The police report estimated she had been buried for two days. When I first saw her, over a month after her attack, she still had fragments of gravel imbedded in her skin.

I was called in to consult when her pregnancy test came back positive. She had stabilized from her injuries, but her eyes were empty, as though something inside her had died. But the ultrasound showed that something inside her was very much alive—a fetus the size of a fingertip, its heart beating rapidly. I took an extra photo for the patient. She looked at it with apathy. As I was leaving the room, I saw she'd dropped it on the floor. I didn't bother picking it up.

It had been three years since I'd delivered my first baby as a third year medical student. Two years of intense textbook training had ended, and finally I was caring for patients. The pinnacle of that wonderful year came the moment I delivered my first baby. I looked down at the new life I held in my hands, and I knew in that instant that I wanted to be an obstetrician.

No one seemed more deserving of care than mothers-to-be and helpless babies waiting to be born. Birth was one of the rare happy events at the hospital, and in those intoxicating years as I finished up medical school, the hospital became for me a holy place. Here came people in need, searching for help, and here gathered the nurses and physicians and medical staff, all working together, dedicated to the high purpose of healing all those who arrived at the hospital doors.

For those who seek healing, Grady is indeed holy ground.

But after a year of internship, the hospital didn't seem so holy anymore. In that year alone, I delivered hundreds of babies, scrubbed on scores of operations, and treated thousands of patients. Little by little, my joy in witnessing the miracle of birth was diminished by the growing realization that many of the newborns I was delivering did not have promising futures. Sometimes it seemed that all those babies healthy enough to survive would be dropping out of school in fifteen years, having or fathering their own babies, going on welfare, and getting addicted to drugs.

Treating patients at Grady was like trying to hold back the tide. No matter what you did or how hard you tried, patient after patient continuously washed up on Grady's shore. As I fought to save the patients, I myself was beginning to drown. By the time I met that rape victim, I had treated more than five dozen rape victims in that year alone. I had come to believe that God had abandoned our hospital for places with more promise.

It was toward the end of my second year of residency that He sent me a lifeboat.

I was seeing patients in the post partum clinic when a young mother wheeled her baby into my office. Her bright smile lit up the room. She looked too healthy to lay claim to the medical chart with her name on it: it was thick as a telephone book.

I flipped to her "footprint" sheet, dated twenty years before, the day she was born. She had been coming to Grady her entire life. I waded through the sheaves of paper until I came to the most recent year. A long stay in intensive care accounted for the thickness. Suddenly I realized that I knew her. She was that patient—the patient who had been brutalized and buried alive. I flipped through the rest of her chart in astonishment that this healthy-looking young woman was the girl with the dead eyes. Sure enough, there was the ultrasound photo I'd taken almost a year ago.

Her smile broadened at my expressions of shock. She told me about her life. The youngest of seven children, all with different fathers, she grew up in a series of foster homes. She ran away at fifteen, living on the streets, prostituting herself for money. She remembered only some parts of her attack, her assailants throwing her into a hole and covering her with dirt. The next thing she remembered was the moment she awakened at Grady Hospital a month later. But things had changed since then, she said. She was off drugs; she was getting her G.E.D. And she was happy.

How did this happen?

She pulled a creased photo from her wallet and handed it to me, eager to share her secret. "This saved my life. When I looked at this, I just knew that no matter what I done, God loved me."

It was the ultrasound photo.

She cradled her baby like a treasure in her arms. She looked down at her daughter and cooed, playing with the pink ribbon in the little girl's hair. "I am... a Mother." Her voice cracked on the word "Mother." It was her answer to everything that had come before. She had given life to a newborn, and her newborn had given life back to her.

All of a sudden the Sacred entered the room, the Holy returned to the hospital. What was this sensation I was feeling? It was Hope, it was Faith, and it felt wonderful. I knew then that I would survive. I would be grateful again to be a physician in this privileged place.

When she got up to leave, the proud mother hugged me. "Guess my baby's name," she said, smiling expectantly. She held the infant up so I could see her soft brown eyes and curls. This was the face of Hope, and yet also a daily reminder of her suffering, the rock bottom of her life—the offspring of a brutal attack.

I couldn't just guess, so I waited patiently until she finally relented. Her eyes glowed with a light I will never forget.

"Miracle. I named my baby Miracle."

The Correct Dose

In my second year of residency, there came a day when I couldn't take it any longer. I told my patient Danielle exactly what I thought. I pounded my fist on the table, jabbed the air with my index finger inches from her forehead, and unloaded a full round of anger and frustration in her face. Then I stormed off, exhilarated, like the winner of a street fight.

It dawned on me as my pulse rate came back down that I would probably be fired. But I was too tired and burned-out to care much.

The second year of the Ob/Gyn training program at Grady Hospital required 80 to 100 hours of work a week. Downtime was a nap in the call room, and socializing was a conversation about stopping blood loss. The strict quasi-military hierarchy that dominated the training program meant that you started at the bottom—and felt it. The stress and pressures of the operating room produced a toxic work environment, where human beings were rude, demanding, and dysfunctional.

Sad to say, I fit right in.

During my month in high risk obstetrics, I found myself for the first time with a patient on the psychiatric ward. The psych ward was its own world, quite separate from the rest of Grady Hospital. The first thing I noticed was that the attending physician actually asked my name and where I was from. I was confused for a moment, then realized what was happening: I was having a civilized conversation.

I next noticed that the psych ward doctors were all well-groomed and appeared well-rested. With no impending medical emergencies, they could spend morning rounds indulging in prolonged intellectual discussions such as you might overhear in an Ivy League dorm. Dressed in my customary blood-stained surgical scrubs, bleary-eyed and disheveled, I began to wonder if I'd missed my calling.

I quickly discovered that I had not.

My pregnant patient—Danielle—had been a heroin addict for more than a decade. She mentioned it repeatedly in an effort to persuade me to prescribe her more methadone, an alternative narcotic given to heroin addicts. Well-spoken and highly intelligent, Danielle complained of so many different psychological symptoms that the psychiatrists couldn't agree on a diagnosis. The month she was under my obstetrical care, her medical chart grew progressively thicker as the psychiatrists added their long, detailed notes. They increased her dose of methadone almost daily until I recommended they stop for the sake of the pregnancy.

"I need more to hold me," Danielle complained. "My dose was almost twice as high when I was pregnant ten years ago." I explained that the baby inside her body was now also addicted. It would suffer unimaginable withdrawal symptoms after its birth. But, Danielle argued, her other baby had done just fine.

I thought about Danielle a lot. Why, after delivering a baby addicted to narcotics ten years ago, was she still a heroin addict? Was drug abuse really the incurable disease to which the psychiatrists had surrendered her? Her chart portrayed her as a victim with a sickness, suffering from childhood angst. Nowhere to be found were words suggesting responsibility, or right versus wrong.

Danielle made my blood boil. I struggled to maintain a proper professional distance.

Residency training was an assault on my soul, for many reasons. But the worst part was witnessing the plight of innocent babies. I'd sweat and struggle to bring a beautiful baby safely into the world, only to send the newborn home with a mother you wouldn't trust with a houseplant.

I had to believe there was some hope, so I tried a different strategy with Danielle. I brought an ultrasound machine to the psychiatry floor. I wanted to show her the beautiful human being growing inside her body. I wanted Danielle to know that her decisions were affecting someone else. I spent thirty minutes on the ultrasound and gave her a dozen photos. I thought I caught a glimpse or two of a caring, expectant mother in her face. But as I was leaving, she pleaded, "I just need something more to hold me."

An emotional volcano suddenly erupted inside of me. Never before had I raised my voice with a patient, but I began to yell at Danielle, and once I'd begun, I was afraid I could never stop. "These psychiatrists may be interested in what you have to say!" I shouted. "But I'm not a psychiatrist and I'm not interested in hearing all your psychobabble! That baby inside of you is as much my patient as you are—he's the only reason I'm here! And you're hurting that innocent child. You need to SHUT UP and change your life!"

Once again, I found myself going through the rest of the day's work half-expecting to be fired—a humiliating, dream-destroying prospect. At least, I thought cynically, I'd finally be able to catch up on sleep.

The next morning, however, I still had a job. More remarkably, I discovered on my next visit to Danielle that my patient had gone through some sort of metamorphosis. Instead of running her mouth, and pestering me for methadone, about all I could get out of her was "Yes, sir," and "No, sir," and "Thank you, Dr. Litrel." She was like that for the rest of my month on that rotation. I was intrigued but suspicious. How to account for her behavior? Maybe she was just frightened for her life.

A few weeks after her discharge Danielle showed up at the obstetrical clinic, refusing to see any doctor but me. I couldn't tell if I should feel honored or annoyed.

Her remaining prenatal appointments passed uneventfully. I didn't deliver her baby, but the day after the birth, I took great pleasure in honoring her request to tie her fallopian tubes. I cut them, tied them, burned them—everything short of throwing them on the floor and stomping on them.

Danielle's baby, as I expected, required a prolonged hospitalization for methadone withdrawal. As had happened with her first baby, Danielle lost the child to foster care. Her social services case worker assured me Danielle would never regain custody of her child.

Several months later, I couldn't believe my eyes when I happened to glance out my clinic window and saw Danielle on the sidewalk in front of the hospital, pushing a baby carriage. The system had failed, again. Why was I surprised? Danielle always had been a good talker.

I brooded on this for a few minutes. What kind of mother does a heroin addict make? Then I shook it off. No sense crying over spilled milk.

Two years later, Danielle surprised me again. She returned to my clinic with her young son. She wanted me to know that she had a good job and had been off all drugs for almost a year. She thanked me for caring about her during her pregnancy. She even thanked me for getting angry with her.

"But you know," she said triumphantly, "you were wrong all along, and I was right. I really did need more to hold me."

My mouth opened involuntarily, to say God-only-knows-what. But before I could get any words out, I noticed that Danielle's intelligent eyes had a twinkle in them. She picked up her son, who threw his arms around her neck. Danielle closed her eyes and held him close for a long moment.

She opened her eyes and gave me a sober, knowing look. "You know, Dr. Litrel…." She paused to take a breath and collect herself. "After all these years, I think I'm finally on the correct dose."

A Broken Heart

My patient Tina's five-year-old boy sat with his eyes glued to an episode of *Sponge Bob Square Pants* on the television set. Just behind him in the hospital room his mother was going through all the travails of labor. The child seemed oblivious to his mother's excruciating pain and the impending birth of his younger sibling.

Sponge Bob is a cartoon character made of sponge who wears square pants because he is, well, square. He lives in an undersea community with his fellow invertebrates. In this particular episode, one of the other characters was bullying Sponge Bob. Quivering with fear, Sponge Bob closed his eyes in expectant terror. But when the bully's blow came, Sponge Bob didn't feel a thing. He is, after all, made of sponge. The bully persisted in his futile and increasingly frantic efforts to inflict pain, punch after punch, until he finally passed out in exhaustion. An untroubled Sponge Bob went on about his daily routine. Tina's son squealed with laughter.

Tina had another contraction. As it peaked she began to cry out in agony. The epidural wasn't working well. "This is my last pregnancy," she declared between groans. "I'll never do this again. I can't believe how much this hurts!" She had been complaining about a hot spot and was acutely tender on one side. It made her labor feel like a branding iron was being pressed into her. "I can't stand this! Why does it hurt so much this time?"

Trying to distract her with humor, I feigned confusion. "Oh, you wanted an epidural on BOTH sides of your body?"

That sort of comment may come back to haunt me years later when I'm sitting by myself wondering why my patients have stopped coming to see me. To her credit, Tina managed a wan smile, understanding that we both needed a diversion and I needed to create some objectivity in the face of the fetal heart monitor. The baby's heart tracing showed that the baby was struggling.

Three years before, I had delivered Tina's last baby after a perfect labor. By "perfect" I mean that the infant's heart rate was reassuringly normal throughout and that Tina was never in significant pain. In the early hours of the morning, she delivered without a sound, making not even enough noise to rouse her family, who were sprawled asleep around the room.

Tina hadn't wanted to wake anyone. She smiled mischievously, like a child opening Christmas presents without permission. When I insisted that a family member should do the ceremonial cutting of the cord, she volunteered to do it herself. I handed her the scissors, and for the first and only time in my career, the mother cut her own umbilical cord.

It was a healthy baby boy with an angel's face. Looking into those clear eyes was like peering through a window into the heart of God. He began to cry softly, awakening his family to the startling discovery that the big moment had arrived and they had missed it. It seemed the perfect beginning to a beautiful young life.

Ten days later, he died.

An infection was listed as the final cause on his death certificate, but Tina's son died of a broken heart—it was made wrong. The condition is called transposition of the great vessels—the arteries leaving the heart are connected to the wrong chambers. Throughout Tina's pregnancy and labor, there had been no hint of trouble. But after her little boy was born and had to rely on his own body for survival, the secret of his broken heart was revealed.

He was transferred to a children's hospital for a corrective surgery called a switch procedure—the aorta and the pulmonary artery are disconnected from the heart and the vessels switched around. It's as complicated as it sounds, but in the hands of an expert pediatric cardiothoracic surgeon, nine out of ten babies survive. One doesn't.

Losing a child can shatter a mother's life, emptying her soul of joy for the rest of her years. Tina was devastated. But in the following months her depression lifted, as she drew strength from her faith and spiritual courage. I watched her fight her way through the grief and was filled with admiration and humility, doubting that when my time comes, I will be as brave.

God makes our bodies. We cannot choose the physical framework of our hearts. But we *are* free to choose its spiritual makeup. Tina chose to trust God and accept the pain as well as the joy He had given her. I have seen many people fixate on their suffering, stumbling through life like victims of violent crime, fearful and flinching at loud noises.

Even I flinched in fear when, a year later, Tina's pregnancy test came back positive. For nine months I kept her in my sights. One ultrasound after another revealed a perfect heart inside her baby. But the memory of her loss still worried me. For 40 weeks she had a very uptight doctor, and when she went into labor and the baby's heart rate was less than perfect, she had to endure my feeble jokes about her epidural.

I helped pull out her baby—another angelic boy. As his strong cry filled the room, I knew that not only the mother, but the child, too, had been blessed with a strong, healthy heart.

Later, while I filled out the paperwork, her five-year-old lost interest in the miracle of birth and turned once again to the television set. Another episode of *Sponge Bob Square Pants* had the boy's laughter filling the room.

I thought about Tina's second child and the trauma of her loss, and about her newest child and the pain of the labor. It would be useful to be like Sponge Bob, made of sponge and impervious to all pain, taking punch after punch from life with an unwavering smile.

The worst blow of all is grief. When we extend our hearts in love, we don't just risk terrible suffering, we guarantee it. Our time here together will end. But whether we get ten days or ten decades, our lives on Earth are a mere instant in eternity. Yes, the body is mortal, but the soul lives on. As frightening as it is to love, to risk loss and the certain ache of grief, it is the only choice. Only when you choose faith will you hear the immortal heartbeat of the soul.

A "Celestial Discharge"

As part of my residency training, I spent three months on Grady's general medicine wards. Even the internal medicine residents, who actually belonged there, hated working the Grady wards. The hours were long, the patients were often seriously ill, and staff members were constantly battling each other. The typical Ob/Gyn resident, like myself, taken away from Labor and Delivery and the Operating Room, hated it even more.

So I couldn't help sulking when I met with the internal medicine intern to receive his notes on the patients I was taking over. With a growing smile of relief, he handed me the cards, one by one, detailing each patient's history and clinical course. As he approached the bottom of the deck, his smile became a broad grin that threatened to run out of room on his face. *His* Grady month was over. Hurray! Hurray! Hurray!

I wanted to punch him in the nose.

The last patient he signed out to me was a man in his mid-thirties dying of AIDS. His history filled three cards, each written in the hand of a different doctor. The man was a "Rock," the intern remarked. A "Rock" was Grady vernacular for a patient you couldn't get off your service. His medical problems were unsolvable, too serious to send him home. The Grady wards were full of Rocks. They ate up your time and emptied you of hope.

I became this man's fourth doctor. For more than two months, the intern explained, they had been waiting for his "Celestial Discharge"—medical slang for death. It had been two years since I'd last heard the expression as a third year medical student working on the wards. The intern under whom I had worked at the time was quite charismatic, skilled at camouflaging his compassion with macabre humor. Whenever a difficult "Rock" died, he would ceremonially kiss his first two fingers and lay them on the patient's card.

"The Kiss of Death," he'd solemnly announce. Then he'd rip up the card, toss the pieces into the garbage, and cheerfully declare, "Another Celestial Discharge!"

His antics were unprofessional. But the futility of caring for dying people can cause even the most hopeful soul to collapse. And like the dark humor portrayed by the character Hawkeye in M*A*S*H, his wisecracks sometimes provided the only fuel to keep the rest of us going.

I worried about becoming that jaded intern with the well-honed wit. Clutching the stack of tattered cards that represented my new patients, I made my way around the wards, saving the AIDS patient for last. As an intern passing through the wards for just a month, I'd have to find a way to get around his nurses if I intended to actually do something for him.

Most of the nurses at Grady Hospital were competent and professional, and a few were simply superb. Nursing tends to attract the kindest and most compassionate people you'll ever meet. But a veteran Grady ward nurse with decades in the trenches is not about to take orders from a fledgling intern. I wasn't too surprised when the AIDS patient's nurse refused to get up from her desk and leave her fashion magazine to find his chart for me. "Busy," she snapped.

I tracked down the chart and set out down the hall to see my patient.

He was as shriveled as a victim in a concentration camp, emaciated beyond comprehension. I found him in a fetal position, too weak to answer my knock. I introduced myself and he simply nodded. His lips were parched, his voice too weak for me to hear, and he looked at me with vacant eyes.

I sat on the chair at his bedside and read his chart. It

told an epic tale of illness and suffering. His most recent problem was a herpes lesion on his backside, for which he was on intravenous antiviral medication, plus the multiple medications that made up his AIDS cocktail. Reluctantly, he agreed to let me see it.

He convulsed in pain as I tried to open his diaper. Very slowly I pulled it back. His body shook and he wept dry tears of agony. I held his rough bony hand to try to comfort him. His long yellowed fingernails dug weakly into my palm, and I squeezed back.

When I looked, I had to stifle a gasp—an angry sore, larger than a record album, covered his entire backside. Bright red with a white border, it resembled a giant cold sore covering twenty percent of his body. The hideousness of it overwhelmed me.

Back on the first day of my internship, dressed in my crisp new white jacket with my name embroidered on the pocket, I had proudly stared at myself in the mirror, convinced I was going to be the best doctor there ever was. I was determined to always demonstrate the highest degree of professionalism. I would always conduct myself with patients, nurses, and other doctors in such a way as to be worthy of their admiration.

I was full of myself.

But staring at that man's bottom, I crumbled. I had no idea what to say to this human being. His nightmare was beyond both my reach and my imagination.

He had likely gotten infected through sex or shooting up drugs. Now, he had been abandoned. No one had visited him during his entire stay. I couldn't help judging him, as if he somehow deserved it, that maybe this was a just punishment for choosing an unhealthy life style. That might have made me feel better. But as I stared in stunned silence at his enormous ulcer, I knew that no one deserved what he had to endure. I wanted to be a good doctor and help this man. But my brain had stalled.

Finally, I found my voice. "I am so sorry.... I have no idea what to do for you. No one should suffer as much as you are." He gave my hand a weak squeeze and a look of gratitude crossed his face. He tried to speak, but I had to lean down close to hear.

He was asking for pain medication. Of course, I assured him. Back at the nurse's station I scanned through his medication list. I was horrified to find that during his entire hospitalization not one of the exhausted residents who had been assigned to his care had bothered prescribing anything for pain. I felt guilty, and worried that I was no better than any of my fellow doctors—just another exhausted resident too tired to relieve the suffering of another human being. Had I ever made the same omission myself? I realized I would never know.

I asked the nurse why he had never been given anything

for pain. She shrugged apathetically: "He never asked."

I scribbled out an order for morphine and then hovered over the nurse to make sure she got it. I went back and reassured my patient that I would see him first thing in the morning. I was not going to be one of those interns who had neglected him.

That night he died.

When I found out the next morning, I was grateful—for both of us.

That was more than a decade ago, and since then tens of thousands of patients have come under my care. But in my mind's eye, I have always seen this patient clearly, felt his bony fingers with nails like claws clinging to my hand. The memories have plagued me, and it's been a constant battle with guilt and doubt. A hundred times I've asked myself: Why did he linger? And why did he die under *my* care?

Finally, one day, an answer dawned on me—maybe he had just been waiting for a friend.

Your Dreams are the Voice of God— So Listen Up

- *The White Coat* -

- *Audible Bleeding* -

- *A Dream to Fly* -

"Your vision will become clear only when you look into your heart....
Who looks inside, awakens."
–Carl Jung

"We both had dreams," they answered,
"but there is no one to interpret them."
Then Joseph said to them,
"Do not interpretations belong to God?
Tell me your dreams."
–Genesis 40:8

There has been an explosion of knowledge in modern biology, driven by our understanding of the theory of evolution and what we have learned about DNA. We're told that trillions of cells make up the body we see in the mirror, and that inside each and every one of these cells is the complete DNA blueprint for building the entire body. In other words, a skin cell has all the information needed to build the liver. A heart cell has all the information to build the skeleton. A cell you cannot even see without a microscope contains all the necessary information for our complete biological creation.

Fervent Christians throw up their hands in dismay at all this and decry the relentless voice of science. Scientists throw up their hands in incredulity at Christian doctrines. The clinician, trying to heal his patients, knows that both have merit.

Faith and science are different models for understanding the same truth.

No anatomy textbook describes the structure or location of the human soul. What is its blood supply? What ligament system holds it in place? This omission can lead the student of medicine to believe the soul does not exist, and that even if it did, its existence would have no bearing on the health of the human body. In truth, the reason for the omission is that the soul cannot be detected with our "primitive" technology, just as before the invention of the microscope, the cell could not be observed.

We know our lives have spiritual purpose. We feel it even though we cannot see it. If we could look inside the soul we would see God's blueprint for our spiritual lives. He has provided us with hopes and dreams to guide the growth of our souls, just as He provided DNA to guide the growth of our bodies.

The White Coat

I was a seven-year-old hunting frogs on vacation with my family when I cut my leg badly. In knee-deep water in a Vermont swamp I collided with something sharp and painful. I raised my foot and found muscle and bone protruding through a gaping hole in my calf, blood cascading down my leg.

I ran back to our cabin in breathless terror and when my mother saw the bloody mess my leg had become, her usual stoicism became panic. She quickly wrapped my leg with a towel, put me in the car, and drove pell mell down the narrow farm roads to the closest medical facility open that Sunday morning—the office of a country doctor.

He could have been a model for Norman Rockwell. His

white coat, gray hair, and gentle smile immediately stilled my fears. Up to that point, my impressions of most strangers had been that they were untrustworthy. Growing up in Long Island with my Asian mother and Italian father, I had often felt like a mutt in a shop full of pedigrees. My almond eyes and dark skin attracted the attention of other children and their parents. From the former I received taunts, from the latter, pointed inquiries about my heritage. Strangers were people who some-times poked fun and always made me feel uncomfortable.

But this stranger in the white coat seemed benign, almost angelic. As he numbed and cleaned my wound, he explained in gentle tones what he was doing. I watched in fascination. By the time he had finished stitching, I knew that I wanted to grow up and help people, just as he was doing. I wanted to be part of this magical world where people loved and cared for each other, regardless of how they appeared or where they had come from.

I wanted to be a doctor.

Two decades later, I was in my third year of medical school and on my way to achieving my boyhood dream. My classmates and I had immersed ourselves for 70 hours a week, week after week, in our textbooks, in the study of disease and the human body. Armed with my vast knowledge, I was eager to proceed to the next step—clinical training at Grady Hospital in downtown Atlanta. On the holy ground of this teaching hospital, I would heal the sick, save lives, stamp out disease and suffering. Soon I would become a doctor in a white coat—someone who treated all strangers as friends.

However, reality was sobering. I quickly discovered that like all my fellow students, I had no idea what I was doing. I didn't just feel like an idiot—I *was* an idiot. Forget about stamping out disease. I couldn't even draw blood.

Nowhere did I feel more incompetent than on Trauma Surgery. My job was to shadow the third year surgery resident, a harried physician doing his surgical training after medical school. One Saturday night, a thin, inebriated African American named Mr. Stanton became our biggest problem. He'd found himself on the losing end of a knife fight.

Mr. Stanton had multiple stab wounds in his chest and abdomen. The stretcher and sheets were covered with blood. He thrashed around so much we had to tie him down. When the nurse, a seasoned pro, stuck his arm to place another IV, he cursed and tried to bite her. She casually moved aside to avoid him.

The idealistic rookie, I was stunned. The surgery resident simply shrugged: "Just another member of the Grady Gun and Knife Club."

Mr. Stanton needed surgery, but he wouldn't consent. Each time the resident attempted to explain why he should, Mr. Stanton cut him off with violent cursing and a ferocious glare. Precious minutes passed, and finally the resident gave up. He called the Chief Surgical Resident.

The Chief had been sleeping and was annoyed. In his final year of training, the Chief would normally be allowed to doze peacefully in the call room until the lower residents had a patient prepped and in the operating room. But, like every committed surgeon, he enjoyed surgery, and Mr. Stanton was a good case. The maxim of surgery is, "A chance to cut is a chance to cure."

So the Chief personally tried to convince Mr. Stanton. "What do you mean you won't sign the consent? If you don't have surgery, you will DIE! You're bleeding inside—you'll be dead tonight!" Mr. Stanton responded with another barrage of profanity.

The Chief looked at me. "You! Mr. Medical Student!" he barked, not bothering to read my name tag. "Take this *gentleman* to Radiology and get a CAT scan." He handed me a consent form. "And try to get him to sign this. If you do, you save his life."

Alone on the elevator with Mr. Stanton, I became the next victim of his foul mouth. He glared at me, his eyes filled with anger—and something else, too. I pondered for a long minute and it came to me. Mistrust. His eyes were filled with mistrust. How in the world do you get a stranger fresh out of a knife fight to trust anyone?

Then I remembered the knife fight I once got into. I was four years old.

It was my second day of nursery school. On the first day,

the other children had laughed at me. My Asian appearance made me an obvious target for ridicule. Why were they making fun of the way I looked? I was confused and frightened by the teasing. I was also infuriated.

The next day I sneaked a butter knife to school. When the children started in again, I pulled out my knife. My fellow pre-schoolers screamed in terror. An exhilarating sense of power filled my entire being, for five seconds. Then the teacher arrived and I was disarmed. My mother was called, I was taken home, and my bottom was spanked. That was my first and last knife fight.

But the incident did leave a wound. I never looked at myself in the mirror the same way again. I had discovered that I looked different, and I hated it. I hungered to escape my skin. I longed to look like the people all around me, for my eyes to open wider, for my skin to grow lighter.

Then I met my white-coated hero in Vermont, and it became clear to me, young as I was, that a doctor inhabited a world where prejudice had no voice, where caring came first. In emulating my rescuer, I thought I could get to a place that was colorblind. I thought that, finally, I could escape prejudice once and for all.

Grady proved me wrong. The minute I walked through its doors, I was assaulted by the forces of racism. This time, I wasn't "Chinese." Surrounded by a largely African American staff, nurses, and patient population, I had become something else. I was White.

Grady Memorial Hospital is a stone's throw from Martin Luther King Drive and two blocks from the famous Dr. King's pulpit at Ebeneezer Baptist Church. Its bulk rests in the heart of a city that was once the epicenter of the Civil Rights Movement. But in those momentous days, Grady Hospital had been segregated just like any other institution in Atlanta, housing its white and black patients in separate wings.

The wounds of racism heal slowly, and when I worked at Grady they were still visible, three decades after desegregation. Residents and faculty were primarily white, and the staff and patients, by and large, black. Racial tension was embedded in the hospital's culture and usually came not from the patients but the staff. You can't prove you aren't a racist, and it's hard to work with those who think you are.

I understood Mr. Stanton's mistrust. I had encountered it every day of my life. This inebriated African American, fresh from a knife fight, was not about to sign a consent form allowing white doctors to cut him some more.

I showed Mr. Stanton the CAT scan confirming the life-threatening bleeding. He scowled. As I pushed his stretcher back to the emergency room, a wave of sadness and futility engulfed me. An unnecessary death was about to occur, only because of a lack of trust and understanding.

It was three in the morning. I was dead tired. Mr. Stanton had cursed me so many times that even the compassionate part of me was starting to hate his guts. And that's when inspiration struck.

"Look, Mr. Stanton," I said. "I'm just a medical student and I don't know that much, but these surgeons can really help you, and they *want* to. If you don't sign this consent form you're going to die. But to tell you the truth, I really don't care anymore, one way or the other. If you die tonight, all it means to me…." I paused for effect. "All it means to me, is that I get more sleep."

This time his glare was murderous. But he grabbed the pen from my hand and signed on the dotted line.

Back in trauma, the Chief was amazed. "How'd you get him to do it?"

I hesitated, afraid of what might happen if the truth came out. I could be reprimanded or fail my rotation or maybe even get kicked out of medical school.

"Let's hear it!" barked the Chief.

I told him. The silence that followed was awkward. The Chief and the other surgeons exchanged glances. I couldn't breathe, waiting for the consequences.

Then the laughing began. "You told him you didn't care if he died because you'd get more sleep!" the Chief repeated. "Whoo! Ha, ha! That's the best one I've heard in while." The laughter resurfaced off and on for quite a while, and spirits were very high by the time Mr. Stanton's surgery began. "Okay, Litrel, you saved a life—you get a reward." I got to drain the blood from Mr. Stanton's chest.

Placing a chest tube wasn't all I learned that day. Many of us share wounds not as obvious as those from a knife. For me, it was the childhood pain of racial rejection. But I was reminded that the experience of pain is not necessarily a bad thing, and that my dreams had brought me to a place where I could indeed help a stranger.

God has a plan for each of us. He transforms the pain of our past into a window of understanding. For only when we suffer ourselves, can we understand. And only then, can we help each other.

Audible Bleeding

It was the first day of my internship, July 1, and I was embarking on my four-year residency at Grady Hospital in Obstetrics and Gynecology. Bearing the light green badge which declared me officially a resident—no longer a medical student—I presented myself to Labor and Delivery. I felt a jumble of emotions—confidence, eagerness, and a little fear.

I found out later I was on the right track with the fear part. Terror might have been even more appropriate.

The Labor and Delivery team consisted of four residents: a second year resident, a third year, a fourth year (called the Chief in the final year of training), and me, the lowly intern. My job was to evaluate people in the triage room and decide if they needed to be admitted. If they did, I signed them out to an upper level resident, who would over-see their care and make sure no mistakes were made. I also got to do routine vaginal deliveries and C-sections under the guidance of the Chief.

By lunchtime that first day, I had evaluated a dozen pa-tients and delivered a baby under supervision. As I ran from patient to patient making assessments, my confidence grew. I really was a doctor. This was going to be great.

Less than six hours later I encountered a clue that my next four years might not be all I had dreamed. One of my patients awaiting assessment was unusually agitated.

She had just killed someone. "Yup. I sliced his throat from ear ta ear," she declared. She expressed not a trace of remorse. I realized that the blood covering her clothes and obviously pregnant belly belonged to someone else. Then I noticed that she was handcuffed to the exam table. The two large guards stationed outside the door were not standard fixtures.

Stephanie, the third year resident, suppressed a yawn when I told her what was going on down the hall. "Murder is not clinically relevant. How dilated is her cervix?"

She sent me to the operating room for another delivery. She made no move to follow me to supervise. I asked her if I was to do only my second delivery of internship alone. "What? You still need my help?" she asked incredulously.

Apparently not. "No, I'll be alright."

The baby delivered without difficulty. But the placenta—the organ connecting the baby and mother—didn't follow. I began to worry. The patient began to bleed heavily. I asked the nurse to call an upper level resident. The patient continued to bleed. I called for help again. No one came.

I was surprised. I figured there must be some kind of *serious* emergency going on for no one to respond to my call for help. Maybe a couple of quadruplet deliveries, or a multiple-car accident involving a half dozen pregnant women.

It was up to me to handle the emergency. My heart beat like a drum. I took a deep breath and told myself to relax and be professional. I decided I would manually extract the placenta. I knew that it had to come out for the bleeding to stop. The patient did not have an epidural. When I reached in to extract the placenta, she screamed.

Then the bleeding worsened.

I waited with growing anxiety for someone to answer my pages for assistance. As the patient's husband and the nurse looked on, I desperately pressed down on the patient's uterus in an attempt to slow the bleeding. You could actually *hear* the blood pouring off the operating room table, splashing into a bucket on the floor. There had been a macabre joke that had gone around during medical school—"Audible bleeding is a bad sign."

Now I knew it had not been a joke.

The nurse was growing agitated, too. When a Grady

nurse, impervious to emergencies and jaded after a lifetime on Grady's halls, begins to get nervous, it's a bad sign. She also called for help on the intercom. The patient's husband could tell that things weren't going well.

I began to wonder if becoming a doctor had perhaps been a flawed career move. At that moment I could have been quietly and serenely shuffling papers at a nice desk in a freshly pressed shirt and tie, not standing in a cold operating room, clothes and shoes covered with blood, desperately trying to save a woman who was rapidly slipping into shock.

Finally I heard voices in the hall. Help had arrived! I could hear William, my Chief Resident, and Dr. Morgan, the attending professor on call, speaking together just outside the door. I assumed they were wrapping up the emergency matters that had been occupying their attention the past half hour, but gradually it became evident that the tone of the conversation was decidedly casual—an exchange about call schedules and so on.

I couldn't take it any longer. I opened the door. In the most professional voice I could muster I said, "I could use some assistance here."

Dr. Morgan took one look at me in my surgical gown, soaked in blood, and exclaimed, "Good Lord!"

His next motions, I knew, would be to throw off his jacket, don his scrubs, and rush in to save the patient.

But I was wrong. He gestured to my Chief. "William,

take care of this." And he turned away without so much as a backward glance.

It took some time before William could bring the bleeding under control. "Gosh, Mike, this just isn't normal," he kept saying. He called for surgical instruments I had never heard of and performed a procedure I had never studied. Eventually he stabilized the patient, and the bleeding stopped. She would be fine, but would require a blood transfusion and a prolonged hospital stay.

When I asked William how the other emergencies had gone, he was confused. He had been off the floor attending to administrative duties. Stephanie, the third year resident, had been in charge of labor and delivery.

I found Stephanie eating strawberries in the doctors' lounge, watching her favorite soap opera. Did I want a strawberry, she asked me. No, I said, pointing to my blood-soaked garments. I was going to change. She shrugged her shoulders and resumed watching the TV.

As I changed out of my scrubs in the locker room, I struggled to make sense of what had just happened. It took a few moments to piece it together, and then a wave of anger flooded through me. I had been initiated into residency—the Grady way. Without even checking on the patient, the third year resident had assumed that the intern was just paging for help in a temporary panic and would eventually figure it all out.

At 8 o'clock that night, my first day as a doctor ended. I crawled slowly into my car aching like the victim of a street beating. As I drove home, I realized there was no prettier sight than Grady Hospital, seen through a rear-view mirror.

The road before me was dark, and I had no map to tell me the correct route. Like so many of us, I would not see why I was here until I had the perspective of time, many years later. What did God have in mind for me now?

A Dream to Fly

Shortly after starting my residency program I fell into a very bad mood. It lasted about two years. It reached a record low the day I took over the Emergency Service at Grady Hospital as a third year resident. My patients were a cross section of Atlanta's typical victims of urban violence and despair. There was a pregnant patient who had been shot in the lung. There was a pregnant woman brain dead from a suicide attempt. And there was the usual stuff, too—AIDS patients, miscarriages, surgical emergencies.

One night after an especially difficult shift, I was sitting in a movie theater next to my wife, Ann. I hadn't smiled for months. She was worried about me and tried to encourage me to talk. But the unspoken understanding in residency was,

"Ask for help any time you need it—but it's a sign of weakness." So I found her concern almost an imposition—in fact, quite annoying.

My mind was preoccupied with one of my less-ill patients. I couldn't remember her name, but in the dark theater, I kept seeing her tearful face. The ER had paged me about her just as I was going home. The number of patients in my care was already overwhelming, and the additional case made me angry. The patient was sixteen years old, with pain so severe she could hardly walk. Her problem was obvious—pelvic inflammatory disease. A dozen just like her had come through that month already. She was still sobbing when I left her in the exam room. Back when I was a beginning medical student, I would have taken the time to hold her hand and reassure her. But I was in a hurry with many patients left to see.

My stomach ached by the time the movie ended. The bucket of buttered popcorn I had devoured may have had something to do with it. As Ann and I walked through the lobby, we crossed paths with a clean-cut young man whose face registered a sudden look of recognition. He turned to me as if wanting to speak to me. I plowed ahead, avoiding him as I might a panhandler outside of Grady. But he caught up with us. The young man was a former chemistry student of mine named Thomas.

I had taught high school in Atlanta the year before I started medical school. Like many teenagers, the students in my classroom were a rude and sullen lot. I was an inexperienced teacher and had trouble at first controlling my students. There were outbursts of profane language almost daily. (When the parents finally complained, I promised the principal I would curb my tongue.)

After awhile, I realized my students weren't as evil as I had first surmised. They wanted to have fun, of course, just like we all do. But underneath, they had important concerns about life; they had questions not addressed in the academic curricula, about faith and purpose, and why they were here.

Like so many of us, they felt lost.

So I tried to teach them some of what my parents had taught me—to be grateful for their blessings, to believe in their abilities, and to reach for bigger and better goals. These lessons were surprisingly well received, and my students tried harder to master the science as well. I felt proud to be assisting young minds along what I believed to be a more fulfilling path.

But seven years later, the younger self I remembered from those teaching days seemed naïve. Yes, I had accomplished my goal of becoming a doctor, but Grady Hospital had a way of beating down even the most idealistic person. I felt uncomfortable running into my former student. I was a different person now.

But Thomas had changed, too. He had been a scruffy, skinny teenager more interested in the lunchroom than the lesson. He was like Shaggy, Scooby Doo's best friend. He was bright enough, but my chemistry class was to him a haunted house full of danger. He did just enough to pass.

I was astounded to learn that Thomas had become a pilot for a major airline. *Shaggy* was flying jets? I could picture him fighting over a pizza with his canine co-pilot while they were supposed to be landing the plane. I tried to keep the surprise out of my voice when I asked him just how he had done this.

Thomas said he had always dreamed of flying, but never believed it was possible. "And that's what I came over to tell you, Mr. Litrel. I've been wanting to tell you, you made a big difference in my life. You kept saying we could be whoever we wanted to be." He smiled. "One day it just hit me. I asked myself, 'Hey, why not me?'"

On the way home, Ann and I held hands for the first time in a long while. I lay awake far into the night. I prayed, remembering so many things I had forgotten. We all get lost, sometimes, and lose our faith, lose sight of our dreams. We don't trust in God's plan. We don't do our best, but instead just enough to get by, and our lives don't turn out as we had dreamed. We despair. And the years pass without our really living.

I was on call the next day, another thirty-six hours at Grady. I hadn't slept much, but I felt renewed and energetic. The first patient I saw the next morning was the young woman from the emergency room. She was still tearful, but as we spoke, her tears dried, and in their place shone trust and gratitude. The emergency room paged me—I had another patient to care for.

As I waited for the elevator, I caught a glimpse of my reflection in the stainless steel doors and I hardly recognized myself.

I was smiling.

It Almost Makes You Believe in God

———— ⟫◆⟪ ————

— An Angel in Disguise —

— Almost Makes You Believe —

— No Translator Necessary —

*"A baby is God's opinion that
life should go on."*
–Carl Sandburg, poet

*"What is man that you are mindful of him,
the son of man that you care for him?
You made him a little lower than the angels
and crowned him with glory and honor."*
–Psalms 8:4-5

The practice of medicine calls us each day to witness the glory that is Life. Every child born reaffirms our faith in God and, perhaps, our faith in God's faith in us. Medicine shores up our belief that God created all men equal. He has not altered our anatomy from one race to the next. Rich or poor, beautiful or ugly, black or white, God brings each of us into the world in the same way. He has created us to share the same sorrows, the same joys, the same experiences of birth and death. We are fully human, yet created in the image of the Divine.

Jesus' primary lesson for us was to love—to love our Creator and our fellow man. He didn't preach that we have the right to judge which of our fellow men are to receive our love. Jesus didn't say "Love those with the correct skin color and the correct nationality," and leave us to infer it was okay to hate everyone else.

That was a concept we invented without His help.

Love opens the way to belief. Love is the reason for this glorious journey. When we love most fully, we see most clearly, and God reveals to us His presence, in the face of every person we meet.

An Angel in Disguise

It was Christmas Eve at Grady Hospital, and there were only three of us residents left to work the service. I was in my first year of residency training, working through the required three months on the general medicine wards.

We all wore Santa hats.

The hats were an effort to boost morale as we worked twenty-four hours straight. We had thirty patients, sick with all kinds of conditions—cancer, strokes, heart attacks, pneumonia. One of them, Mr. Teel, was a forty-ish mentally retarded white man. He had been on our service for two weeks, hospitalized for extreme malnutrition. The day he was admitted he weighed seventy pounds.

"Please find out what is wrong with Ralph," his sister

pleaded. "I can't understand why he's lost all this weight." She was under investigation, she told me indignantly, by the State Welfare Office, for suspicion of neglect. "We give him wonderful care," she said. "They should be using their time to find real criminals!"

I reassured his sister we would find out what was going on. She expressed her gratitude and made a point of checking on his progress every day. Her concern was touching, and I enjoyed being in a position to help.

When I checked on Mr. Teel that Christmas Eve, he was doing exactly what he had been doing every day of his hospitalization. Pigging out. He was on a high calorie diet, with supplemental shakes. He drank so many of these that we had to sneak some from the other floors to satisfy his hunger. It was fun, watching him eat all the time. He couldn't talk or understand very much, and he had to wear diapers. But he enjoyed his food. And he was getting better every day.

Mr. Teel had an unpleasant roommate: a prisoner, shackled to his bed, healing from a gunshot wound in the abdomen. This was not an uncommon sight at Grady, but this guy was particularly rough looking. He had bulging muscles everywhere, and his dark skin was plastered with tattoos. He glared at us whenever we entered the room. I was grateful for the armed guard stationed just outside.

We hadn't been able to figure out what had caused Mr. Teel's emaciation. Cancer was the number one suspect.

But all our CAT scans and MRI's had come up short. No tumor anywhere. Mr. Teel's sister arrived on the morning of Christmas Eve, beautifully clothed and bedecked with jewelry. She asked me if we had a diagnosis yet. I told her regretfully that we were still drawing a blank. She insisted on more tests. "I just don't understand it. Why is he so thin? There has to be something wrong with him."

There was something disingenuous in the tone of her voice, and for the first time I felt a flicker of suspicion. The diagnosis clicked. "We've fed him for two weeks," I said, looking straight into her eyes, "and he's gained back a lot of weight. After all these negative tests, I think the problem is he just hasn't been fed enough."

Her face clouded over and she looked away. Then she left the ward, uttering not a word of denial or defense.

It made for a sad Christmas Eve. At Grady, everywhere you turn there is someone suffering. So much of the suffering is unnecessary, and that makes it sadder still. No doubt Mr. Teel was difficult to care for at home. But he could have been placed in a nursing facility. Throughout the long day, I kept thinking about him, a mentally retarded man almost dead of neglect. My Santa hat stayed on my head, but it didn't feel like Christmas. The hospital seemed barren of love.

I stopped by Mr. Teel's room late that night. As I drew close, I heard someone singing "Silent Night." I peeked around the curtain and was astonished. There was the prisoner roommate, singing to Mr. Teel and helping him with his dinner. "Hey Mr. Teel," the prisoner was saying, "you lucked out—look at all the good things you get to eat." His smile lit up the room.

But when he spotted me, the smile vanished. The familiar glare was back. "I'm not doin' nothin'," he growled. "Ain't no nurse around and the man's gotta eat."

I groped for a response. "I appreciate you taking care of him," I said. "We need all the help we can get around here." It felt like Christmas again. I stuck out my hand to shake his. "Merry Christmas, Sir."

He crushed my hand in a friendly way and smiled big. "Merry Christmas, Doc! And I dig the Santa hat."

I gave him the hat. He made a better Santa than I did, I told him.

Of all my Christmas Eves, that one is my most memorable. I witnessed a beautiful sight—a prisoner in chains feeding a starving man deserted by his own family. It was a fitting event to honor the birthday of Jesus, a man who lived among the rejected, offered hope and healing to the poor, and taught us not to judge each other, but to love.

Almost Makes You Believe

After a doctor delivers a hundred or so babies, he or she begins to see the obvious: no matter the color, creed, or culture of the mother, delivering a baby is pretty much the same for everyone. After a few hundred, it's just not that hard.

For the doctor, I mean. The mother still has it rough.

To the mother falls the heroic work of labor—many long hours marked with blood and pain, forcing the baby's head from her body. Once she has reached that point, she has given the doctor only two small tasks: first, pull the baby's head down; then, pull it up. That's obstetrics in a nutshell. Down, up. Always been that way, always will be.

Every year a few new doctors try to innovate. It was July at Grady Hospital, and the intern I was supervising as a third year resident insisted on doing things a new way—the Up First method.

Not only is this impossible, it gives the baby quite a headache.

As I watched the intern fumble, I was a model of patience. Many of my fellow residents had come from Emory's Medical School, where the students deliver Grady babies long before graduation. But this freshly promoted doctor had come from a medical school affiliated with a hoity-toity hospital, chock full of private patients. As a student, she had been allowed to draw blood, maybe, but had never come close to delivering a baby. Her first deliveries had to be more carefully managed than those of the Emory graduates.

"Pull down, Margo, down," I repeatedly whispered in her ear. But Margo kept pulling up. Finally, the baby's head turned purple—a bad sign—and I lost my temper.

I don't remember exactly what I said to Margo as I took over the delivery, placing my hands over hers to direct them downwards and deliver the baby, now floppy in unconciousness. But in that moment of stress, I may have expressed complete disgust with her as a physician and a human being.

Out of the corner of my eye, I watched the pediatricians resuscitate the baby, as Margo and I waited for the placenta to deliver. They were urgently pumping oxygen into the baby's lungs, as it lay ominously still. With the passage of each silent second, I kicked myself for not taking over sooner. Finally, after endless minutes, the reassuring sound of the baby's cry broke the tension. I was happy.

But Margo was not. As she watched the baby come to life, her lower lip began to quiver. Her eyes filled with tears. And she began to sob.

Crying is a summer tradition among the new interns at Grady hospital. One minute you're walking tall, a June medical school graduate with a diploma and the title of Doctor. The next moment you're July's lowly intern—thrown like a juicy piece of meat into the ravenous jaws of a thousand-bed indigent teaching hospital. It's not a question, really, of *whether* you'll break down, but when.

Taking responsibility for Grady's extremely distressed patients is a mind-boggling challenge. As I'd struggled through my own internship, I had noticed that the supervision of a good upper level resident made all the difference. So I'd promised myself that when I was finally an upper level, I would be the model teacher and supervisor.

But now I had become the first upper level to make one of the new interns cry. I regretted the distinction. I hadn't been the biggest jerk in the residency program—just the season's first.

Margo delivered the placenta, her shoulders still heaving with sobs. My sympathy became tinged with resentment.

I'd hardly raised my voice at her. On the Grady Scale of Intra-Resident Abuse, this incident barely rated a 2. This was only her first week. She had 201 to go. In my estimation, she needed to toughen up—preferably instantly. She had a laceration to fix, and the patients were piling up.

I scrubbed out of surgery to round on the other patients, six of whom were in labor. As I waded through the work, I worried some about Margo. To survive Grady, you had to learn quickly—it was sink or swim. One delivery with minor complications, and Margo was blubbering like a baby.

I checked on Margo later and found her at the nurses' station, finishing her paperwork. She didn't look upset—in fact, she was smiling. I ventured an apology. "I'm sorry for yelling, I didn't mean to make you cry."

She looked at me with surprise. "You didn't make me cry, Mike," Margo said. "You were fine."

I looked at her in disbelief. She laughed. She casually grabbed my arm and pulled me into the patient's room. She gestured at the baby, now sleeping peacefully in the hospital crib.

"Seeing a baby being born," she said. "It was just *so beautiful*." She shook her head in wonder and bemusement. Tears twinkled again in the corners of her eyes.

Margo went back to her work and I stood there in momentary confusion, looking at the newborn. It had been four years since I had delivered my first baby, and my life-long desire to be a doctor had culminated in the moment I had helped that first tiny patient into the world. As I had held her in my hands, a tidal wave of wonder and joy had washed over me. In delivering babies, I'd found my destiny.

But now, after so many long hours of work, so many days of simply counting the hours until I could sleep again, so many patients and so much suffering—my thoughts and feelings had changed.

I had changed.

I was an expert, well versed in handling the unfortunate and dangerous circumstances that sometimes occur with deliveries. But like the jaded doorman at New York's Waldorf Astoria, I had lost my first day's enthusiasm. Now I was merely doing my job—opening and closing doors, tipping my hat.

The baby looked around at his new surroundings, seeing light for the first time. Ten fingers, ten toes, no concerns—serenity incarnate. Was it only two hundred and eighty days ago that this human being had been conceived? Was it less than a year ago that the fertilized ovum, a mere particle of dust, had blasted off in an explosion of remarkable transformation?

He, too, had changed.

The nurses in the delivery room were bustling around the young parents, tidying things up. The new father, his jaw still agape with wonder, rubbed his wife's shoulder and held her hand. The exhausted mother looked over at her newborn child, her relief and gratitude almost palpable, her love most certainly so.

I looked around the room and saw a disparate group of human beings—patients, nurses, doctors, all from different places, different backgrounds. There was nothing obvious, really, to unite us, except for this: Love. Together we had borne witness and helped bring new life into this world. A sudden realization made me smile: life is wondrous, if you hadn't noticed lately.

Sometimes, in fact, it almost makes you believe in God.

No Translator Necessary

Spanish was my worst subject in high school. It wasn't that it was especially difficult. I just never studied. Typical adolescent thinking: when will I ever need this stuff, anyway? It's not like I'm moving to Mexico.

I didn't expect that Mexico would move to me.

More than ten percent of the babies I've delivered in Georgia have been born to mothers who don't speak English. Just two days into my residency I came face-to-face with a pregnant Mexican patient who needed an exam and couldn't speak a word of English. Suddenly I realized how stupid I had been for blowing off high school Spanish.

Over the next four years of residency training I picked up some key Spanish verbs, so I could usually get my meaning across: "relax, breathe, push, don't push...." The trouble started when I began private practice in the suburbs of north Atlanta. My Guatemalan patients had no idea what I was saying. It took me more than a year to figure out why.

At first it struck me as peculiar that so many of my patients came from Guatemala. How did so many islanders from the South Pacific end up in North Georgia—swim?

Curious, I consulted an atlas. To my surprise, I discovered that Guatemala is not in the South Pacific at all, but just south of Mexico.

I guess I was weak in geography, too.

Furthermore, it turns out that many Guatemalan villagers don't even speak Spanish, but rather a Native American dialect. Suddenly, I didn't feel as guilty about those C's in high school language class.

One of my Guatemalan patients, Rosa, showed up in my office pregnant. We discovered that her growing fetus had a terrible malformation of the brain, clearly visible on her four month ultrasound. We sent Rosa to Emory for a second opinion to make sure. A specialist in high risk pregnancies confirmed the diagnosis and recommended the pregnancy be terminated as soon as possible. There was no cure. The baby couldn't survive.

We tend to think of pregnancy as a joyful time. The obstetrician shares in that joy, but keeps in mind another truth: it is more dangerous to a woman's health to be pregnant than not. Conditions like diabetes and high blood pressure are just a few of the potential complications. It doesn't make sense to put a woman through the risks of pregnancy if there is no chance the baby will survive.

Such was the case with Rosa and her four month old fetus. Sadly, we agreed with the specialist's recommendation to end the pregnancy and turned Rosa's care over to him. He arranged for her admission to Grady.

A month later I was surprised when a still pregnant Rosa came back to my office. She had decided to let the pregnancy run its course.

Rosa was among those Guatemalans who speaks only the Native American dialect of the region. Helena, Rosa's shy and petite eleven year old niece, was the only translator available. She accompanied her to every appointment. The conversations that followed as a result of this terrible diagnosis would have been difficult enough for an adult, much less a child. But Helena was mature beyond her years, a serious and thoughtful soul. We relied on her completely.

So Rosa's pregnancy continued. At each appointment I expected her baby to have died. A baby with serious malformations will almost always miscarry: miscarriage is God's way of sparing the mother the pain of a full term pregnancy for an unhealthy fetus. However, upon each visit, we found the heartbeat of Rosa's baby still loud and clear. And the unsightly birth defect—Nature so clearly and terribly going astray—became more and more pronounced.

My concern deepened when Rosa's pregnancy began to drive up her blood pressure to dangerous levels. But she steadfastly refused intervention or even blood pressure medication. I couldn't help but wonder if she understood what was going on. If her blood pressure rose to a certain level, she could have seizures and actually experience brain damage herself. I would listen as Helena spoke to her aunt and wonder what was being conveyed. But Helena seemed to understand and share my concerns. She had more trouble explaining her aunt's response.

Rosa went into labor right around her due date. Many immigrants from third world countries are stoic when it comes to pain. A woman who has delivered her last two babies in a hut with a dirt floor often doesn't see the need for all the doctor's care available in America. Rosa was typical. She turned down pain medicine, and labored largely in silence. The baby's head was abnormally enlarged. It was difficult to deliver. Special maneuvers and a very large incision were required.

At last I held Rosa's baby. It was terribly malformed— an enormous head, no eyes, one nostril. As I cut the cord, the baby took one gasp—and died in my hands.

I remember Helena's usually steady voice cracking when she told her Aunt that her baby had died. Rosa bore the news in silence, just as she had labored. We stopped her bleeding and sutured her incision. The nurse washed the baby and gave it to Rosa to hold. The room was silent as I operated. No one said anything. By the time I had finished thirty minutes later, the baby was growing cold.

Afterward, I wondered why Rosa had chosen to go through all this. Why take the path of more pain? Did she not trust our diagnosis? Or was it something else?

An answer came three years later. I was again in the delivery room with Rosa and Helena. This time, Rosa's pregnancy had been entirely uncomplicated. Again she labored quietly without pain medication. The baby came out easily, and I placed her on Rosa's abdomen.

There was silence in the room just as with the first delivery. No noise. No emotions. Like a breath being held. Except this time a baby began to cry softly. It was the high quavering voice of a newborn announcing "I am here, I am here."

Helena smiled. Like sunlight on a cloud, her smile transformed her serious young face. A few seconds later, she broke into laughter: a real child's laugh, the pure and happy laugh owned only by the very young. She quickly stopped as though she were breaking a rule. But she couldn't hide her joy.

Then Rosa, usually stone-faced like so many women from Guatemala, also smiled, despite herself. I watched as she cradled her beautiful baby. She stared at her newborn as though not trusting her eyes. By force of will, I think, she made her smile disappear. I wondered what she was thinking and feeling. It was as though she would not let herself believe in God's gift.

The baby yawned, and finally, for the first time in all her labors of physical pain and thwarted motherhood, Rosa began to weep.

No translator was necessary.

If It Looks Like We Don't Know What We're Doing–It's Because We Don't

———◆►◄◆———

— The Heart Speaks Softly —

— See One, Do One, Teach One —

— An Incompetent Surgeon —

— Searching for a Scapegoat —

— Training Wheels —

"Drop wisdom, abandon cleverness,
And the people will be benefitted
a hundredfold."
–Lao Tzu

"You hypocrite, first take the plank out of
your own eye, and then you will see clearly
to remove the speck from your brother's eye."
Matthew 7:5

When I was a child I thought that doctors were immensely smart and knew exactly what they were doing—performing miracles and saving life after life even before their morning coffee.

The truth is somewhat different. First of all, you drink coffee all the time.

Second of all, you really don't know what you are doing. The responsibilities can be so frightening you are sometimes afraid to admit you don't know what's going on. So you hide behind scientific studies and big words. In addition, the science itself keeps changing, demanding a life-long dedication to study and training.

Yet there is another kind of learning that goes on, with findings unreported in medical literature.

The teachings of medicine, though seemingly irrefutable, are limited. Faith lends a different perspective, bringing order to the unceasing torrent of new research, technological advances, and groundbreaking drugs. Can any textbook ever explain why a single cell smaller than a grain of sand grows over nine months into a newborn baby?

We are lifelong students, with far to go. Jesus taught us that to enter the kingdom of God, we must be like little children. There is nothing to be afraid of: God has given us minds that we may learn, launching into the unknown and encountering new lessons every day. When it comes to living as a human being, there is no such thing as "graduation."

God intends to teach us, if we let Him, all our lives.

The Heart Speaks Softly

My patient was unusually apprehensive before her surgery. The operation would be a simple laparoscopy. Through a small incision under her belly button, I would look inside to diagnose and treat the cause of her increasing pain. The day before, she had been comfortable with our plans for surgery. But that morning she was very frightened and nothing I did could put her at ease. At first she was too embarrassed to tell me why. But finally she admitted she was upset because of a bad dream. She dreamed she was going to die during the operation.

Although the medical literature doesn't support the decision, we postponed her surgery. Her face flooded with relief and gratitude, and I knew it was the right thing to do.

But her husband was angry. The surgery had been planned for a month. He had taken off work and gotten her to the hospital at six that morning. He rolled his eyes in disgust when I told him why I'd cancelled her surgery. Because of a *dream*? Where did I get my medical degree? Voodoo School? He seemed less interested in my explanation and more interested in taking me outside to settle the issue. I became angry and defensive as the insults kept coming, and I started wondering if maybe a fistfight wasn't such a bad idea.

Instead, I told him about Mrs. Strickland.

I met her as a third year medical school student. The Cardiology Chief had told Mrs. Strickland she needed a catheter placed in her heart. But she was frightened and refused the procedure. He considered her too ill to leave the hospital and refused her wishes to be discharged. She had been in the hospital for a week when I met her.

Mrs. Strickland was a pleasant elderly woman, and I was happy with the assignment the Cardiology Chief gave me. "Spend time with her and convince her to get the cath." It was my first year out of the classroom and like other third year students, I was mostly useless to my medical team. The cardiologists were so busy they didn't have the time to spend with Mrs. Strickland. So I welcomed the opportunity to contribute.

I looked forward to our meals together. I could tell our conversations helped her feel better. She had grown up on a farm in northern Georgia but didn't have much family left. She spoke slowly and laughed softly when she shared a pleasant memory. I told her about myself, too, and we became friends.

The Cardiology team was a wonder. Emory University is a cardiology powerhouse, the birthplace of Balloon Catheter Angioplasty. The foremost experts in the world work and train there, performing this marvelous technique. I watched the Cardiology Chief operate on patient after patient, improving life, and holding death at bay. My faith in the life-saving power of technology grew.

Mrs. Strickland did not share this faith. She still refused the procedure. "I think I'm going to die if I have this done," she told me. When I shared her fears with the Cardiology Chief, he became exasperated: "She'll die sooner without it." So I redoubled my efforts to convince her. And after another week, she reluctantly agreed.

I was happy when I wheeled her down to the lab the next morning. At last we could help her. She smiled at me, and I held her hand as she was sedated.

She died on the table a few minutes later.

We had no warning. The procedure had barely begun. Even the Cardiology Chief didn't seem to know what was going on. There was confusion in his voice—and fear. He raced to get her heart beating again. But nothing worked, and the resuscitation became desperate.

Then just as unexpectedly, her heart began to beat again.

Remarkably, the next morning, she was back to her old self. Ashamed that I had so readily dismissed her fears, I had trouble meeting her smile. I began to explain what had happened.

Her next statement stopped me cold.

"I was there, too, you know. I remember everything."

She told me that when her heart had stopped she could see her body lying on the table, with the cardiology team frantically trying to bring her back. She saw me looking very frightened, standing out of the way. But it was peaceful, she remembered, and as she was floating above the room she wondered to herself if maybe it was a good time to die.

"But you've been so nice to me, and I knew it would upset you if I died," she said, holding my hand. "So I decided I wouldn't go just yet."

Dumbfounded, I stared at her in amazement.

Two mornings later we sent her home. "Let's get her out of here before we kill her," the chagrined Cardiology Chief told me. And modern medicine beat a confused but grateful retreat.

I'll always remember Mrs. Strickland and the wonderful gift of her return to life. She was the first patient to teach me humility and show me something the medical literature never could: she taught me to listen, listen carefully, to the heart. It's a mistake to place all of your faith in technology or in the surgeon. The gift of healing is a miracle, like the gift of birth, and the physician is only a witness to this miracle, not the source.

So I finished telling my patient's angry husband about Mrs. Strickland, and again I offered my hand. This time he shook it, and thus we successfully avoided a fistfight. Weeks later, I performed his wife's surgery when she finally felt ready. And, thank God, she was healed.

See One, Do One, Teach One

One of the rotations I did as a third year medical student at Grady was a stint in the Pediatrics ward. The responsibilities were relatively straightforward. The third year medical student examines the dozen or so babies ready for discharge and makes certain all is well. Pretty simple stuff, except when you don't have a clue what you are doing.

Grady Memorial Hospital is reputed to be a teaching hospital. In the years before I entered its hallowed halls, I had imagined multitudes of brilliant professors tirelessly demonstrating clinical techniques to medical students, ensuring perfection in the delivery of care at all times.

Reality somewhat differed.

In most cases, the Grady teaching mantra for medical

techniques was this: "See one, do one, teach one." First see it done. Then do it. Then teach it. But for my first day on pediatrics I wouldn't even get to "see one." I'd be skipping right to the second part—"do one." I arrived at the newborn nursery with a booklet called "How To Do a Healthy Newborn Exam." Its fifty pages described what could go wrong if I missed a diagnosis, outlining case after case with the terrible outcomes that resulted when newborns were sent home prematurely. I resolved to do a great job. I envisioned making a difficult diagnosis, maybe recommending an alternative solution to a pediatrics professor who would nod his head with appreciation—or even admiration.

So I announced my arrival to Mrs. Helen Philpot, the nursery charge nurse. She noted the name badge which marked me as a mere medical student. She rolled her eyes and walked away.

The hardest part of a medical student's job isn't learning the medicine. It's working with the nurses. Each month, before any level of competence is achieved, medical students rotate through different services, while the nurses work on the same service year after year, deepening their experience and skills. That particular eye roll wasn't the first I'd seen, and it wouldn't be the last.

Being incompetent is bad enough. But being treated as incompetent is intolerable. There was only one way I knew to handle the situation.

I took charge. I was authoritative. I dominated. I demanded that Helen get the babies and charts ready for my examinations and waited expectantly for her compliance.

Helen obeyed, glowering. The other nurses looked at me, their eyes full of daggers, but I refused to be intimidated. I swaggered a little as I entered the nursery, exuding self-assurance. This was one third year medical student who knew his stuff.

The babies were all resting in silence, but no sooner had I begun my first exam than the baby began to cry. His voice woke the crowd, and pretty soon a chorus of high pitched wails filled the nursery. I wish I could say their voices were like a chorus of angels from heaven, a reminder of the miracle of life. But the truth is they were making a racket.

A nurse's aide sitting in a rocking chair watched me nonchalantly as she expertly fed baby after baby. Ruby was a mountain of a woman who looked as though she'd been there since the day Grady Hospital opened a hundred years ago. I'd seen her exchange glances with Helen when I'd entered the room. Conscious of her observation, I made sure she saw I knew what I was doing.

It was two hours later when I finally reached the last baby to begin his exam. He was unusually miserable, his face scrunched up and red as a beet. Nothing I did gave him any relief, and he was making so much noise I couldn't listen for heart murmurs. My clinical instincts told me something was very wrong. No baby should cry this much.

I opened the baby's diaper and saw a dressing covering his penis. He had been circumcised the day before. Perhaps there was an infection or undiagnosed trauma. Eager to make the diagnosis, I carefully pulled off the gauze and peered attentively at the area. There was a puzzling string that followed my lifting the gauze. It was attached to his newly circumcised penis. But when the "string" touched my face, I realized it was actually a stream of urine. Flustered, my first instinct was to put the small piece of gauze back where I'd found it. Urine splashed all over. My hand, my sleeve, my lab coat, my glasses—I was soaked.

And then an emergency occurred.

"What's wrong, what's wrong?" Helen Philpot cried, as she rushed into the nursery. I looked around to see her leaning over Ruby, who was holding her chest, stiffening in her chair.

"I… can't… breathe…," Ruby gasped. The other nurses rushed in. "Ruby is a diabetic!" one of them said. "She had a heart attack a few years back."

"Are you choking, Ruby?" Helen asked. Ruby shook her head and pointed at me. Her face was blanching from lack of oxygen. I could see that she wanted my help, and I took out a stethoscope to make an examination. But Ruby's airway suddenly cleared. She took in a deep breath, still clutching at her chest. And then it happened.

Ruby began to laugh. Ruby began to laugh the biggest laugh the world has ever seen. Deep guffaws rolled out of her body as she struggled to explain what had happened. Her hand trembled as she pointed at my urine-soaked front and glasses.

"Oh Doctah!" Ruby said, gasping for breath. "That was the funniest thing I evah did see." Tears streamed down her face, and everyone else, relieved and delighted, was soon caught up in her contagious delight, laughing uproariously as well.

Everyone but me. I was humiliated. So much for being a great medical student. I wanted to explain what I had done, how I'd thought perhaps the "string" might be the source of the baby's discomfort. But as I looked at the sea of faces all laughing with delight, I suddenly realized it was okay if I wasn't perfect. And I began to laugh, too, uncontrollable laughter. Finally, groping for a chair, I collapsed in a paroxysm of cathartic laughing.

It took minutes to recover. During that time one of the nurses took off my glasses and rinsed them in the sink. Helen got a washcloth and scrubbed the urine off my coat. And Ruby rose from her chair and gave me a bear hug. "We love you Doctah," she said to me. "You come back, any time." The other nurses were smiling and nodding, making fun a little, but friendly, too.

The next time I came I brought a box of donuts to share.

We all shared another laugh. It turned out to be a pleasant month of call. And I learned much from folks wiser than me.

An Incompetent Surgeon

After two years of training in obstetrics and gynecology, I had climbed halfway through the ranks of Emory's residency program. My youthful exuberance had been tempered by sobering experience. I had seen thousands of patients, performed hundreds of operations. By mid-year I was on night rotation at Grady, a third year resident supervising and making decisions with hard won know-how.

On one typical evening, a twenty-eight-year-old woman with eight children was awaiting my evaluation. Seven months pregnant, she had been admitted to Grady's high risk obstetrical service because she was in early labor. An ultrasound had revealed twins. With lungs twelve weeks immature, one or both babies could certainly die if they arrived that day.

Before seeing the mother I reviewed her thick chart. She had been only fifteen when she'd had her first baby. She had fired off the next three like a semi-automatic, and they had taken their toll on her body. Succeeding pregnancies had come with complications and early labor.

A wave of annoyance washed over me. It was an emotion I had become familiar with since my arrival at Grady. Part of the annoyance stemmed from the patient being high risk. I would have to watch her even more closely.

In theory, every new patient was an opportunity to learn and grow as a physician, so the more difficult the better. But in practice, after a thousand days of residency, sleep had come to feel a little more rewarding than professional growth.

What really annoyed me was how unnecessary this patient's problems were. Why not stop at four children, or six? Why *nine*? Was she trying for a baseball team?

The official goal of obstetrics is to ensure that every child is well born. "Well born" is a concept that extends beyond ensuring simply the physical health of baby and mother. The health of the family unit is essential as well—the physical, emotional, and financial ability of the family to care for the child.

How could a single mother on welfare take care of eight children? And now she was pregnant yet again, with twins to boot. Who was taking care of the other eight while she was stuck here in the hospital?

If you haven't noticed, many physicians are cold and distant. Before I started medical school I thought they were this way because they were all so smart they couldn't relate to anyone else.

I couldn't wait to join them.

I was disappointed when this proved not to be the case. It turns out the distance is really an emotional protection. After a physician encounters human suffering a few hundred times, he begins to insulate himself from emotional upheaval by erecting barriers between himself and his patients. The suffering of patients presents itself in so many forms, so much of it unnecessary. It hurts to see. Thoughts about this woman's impoverished children would break my heart if I let them.

I tried to think analytically. After an exam, I could see that my patient and her unborn twins weren't in imminent danger. So I broached the topic of prevention—why not prevent this from happening again? I asked her if she had ever considered a tubal ligation.

"I *was* tubalized—last year!!!" she spat, sounding as annoyed as I. I re-examined her abdomen, and there under her belly button was a well-healed incision. My annoyance took a new direction—toward whatever fool of a surgeon had tied her tubes.

Tubal ligations, it's true, can fail. But the odds of getting pregnant with fraternal twins after a tubal are one in ten thousand. It had to be the surgeon's fault. He or she had undoubtedly mistaken the round ligament for the fallopian tube. It's pretty easy to do. But the surgeon must also have neglected to check the pathology report to discover the mistake. And *that* is bad medicine.

I had always prided myself on my surgical skills. Keen observation, calm actions, and conscientious follow-up are the hallmarks of a good surgeon. I tried to live up to those ideals. It takes a lot of doing, and there were more than a few surgeons around who just didn't live up to those standards. Hot on the trail of the unknown culprit, I looked up the operative report. I needed to know who it was.

But when I finally found the name of the idiotic, incompetent fool on the operative report, I realized it was a surgeon I had not considered.

It was me.

My hands shook as I pulled up the pathology report. Could I possibly have missed her tubes? Was this twin pregnancy my fault? Did I allow this mother to give birth again, lying in a hospital unavailable to her other eight children? Was it I who was the incompetent?

Relief washed over me when I saw the report: I had done the surgery correctly. Sometime within the next few days I confessed to my patient just exactly who her surgeon had been. She was pretty cheerful, considering. My attempts to vindicate myself with explanations about medicine and failure rates didn't make much of an impression. As far as she was concerned, it was God's will, and she would live with it.

My patient and her babies did well. Six months after their birth I operated again. Looking at the condition of her tubes, I saw that there was no way she should have conceived. But I removed the remaining segments and offered her double protection with birth control pills.

She gladly accepted.

I still don't know how she defied the odds with her twin pregnancy. No answer, I suppose, is better than my patient's. God creates Life, His miraculous gift to us. And in the same way a tree blossoms with flowers and leaves each spring, a woman's body often blossoms with the miracle of life.

No matter how much a surgeon—incompetent or not—says it won't.

Searching for a Scapegoat

As a physician in private practice, I enjoy going to the hospital in the middle of the night. It reminds me of my childhood conception of the old family doctor, galloping under the stars to reach a neighbor in need. But I also enjoy sleeping in a warm, soft bed. So there is a transition period, the time between waking up and being under the stars when, half asleep and fumbling around, I can be a tad bit grumpy. The fault, I'm sure, rests in my genes; it's a trait I share with both my father and my son Tyler.

It was two in the morning when a hospital nurse named Susie called: she wanted to give my patient a routine medication. I was annoyed she'd awakened me for something trivial, but I bit my tongue. Then she told me another patient had just arrived in the emergency room; she'd have to call back when she knew more. Grumpily I thought, why hadn't she gathered this information before calling in the first place? I expressed my dissatisfaction with her organizational skills in what I thought was an appropriate manner. The next thing I knew, she was expressing her dissatisfaction with me in what I thought was an *in*appropriate manner. My adrenaline surged and I brought a quick end to the conversation. My goal was to go back to sleep, not argue.

But it was too late. My pulse was pounding. So for the next thirty minutes, I lay awake wondering who had come to the emergency room. Two pregnant patients in our practice concerned me: one with twins and the other with an abnormally positioned placenta. Could it be one of them? I called back. My patient was in active labor, but fortunately she was not at high risk. So I took a shower, got dressed, and in no time, was under the stars.

However, I was still irritated with Susie when I arrived at Labor and Delivery, and I decided to give her some grief. She shared with me another piece of her mind. In her opinion, I had attacked her, and she had a right to defend herself. This, of course, was nonsense. I hadn't attacked her. When I had called her telephone strategy "lame," it was in the most professional and matter-of-fact way. It was constructive criticism, that's what it was.

"You are always so grumpy," Susie continued, and then

added a kicker. "Of all the physicians, you have the worst reputation for waking up at night."

This was exaggeration, pure and simple. I couldn't be the worst. Dr. So-and-so made the bad mood into an art form. I knew in my heart I couldn't be worse than Dr. So-and-so. Then Susie delivered a clairvoyant blow—"You're even worse than Dr. So-and-so."

Stunned, I tried to organize my defense—I'm the second worst, I'm only the second worst.... But then something occurred to me. Someone's got to be at the bottom of the barrel; it might as well be me. Other physicians feel the same frustration I do when they are awakened unnecessarily. Some strange force must block them from adequately expressing these feelings. Let's call it good manners. But am I really responsible for my behavior when I am half asleep? If it were Mother Teresa herself, waking me to witness a miracle, I'd still be annoyed.

But I looked at Susie and knew she was even more upset than I was. Her blue eyes flashed with anger, and I could tell I was no longer held in high favor. This was an important realization. On some level, I had always assumed I was universally loved and respected by everyone around me and that any annoying idiosyncratic behavior of mine, such as my reputed late night surliness, was cheerfully accepted as part of my irresistible charm. And I was surprised, too. Susie and I had never before had so much as a disagreement. Why was she suddenly angry with me? But as the conversation progressed, it was evident that indeed, unbeknownst to me, we had argued before—a fair amount, it would seem.

It wasn't the first time I had failed to realize I was having conflict with another person. Ann and I had been married for years before I knew. It's not my fault, really. She expresses her irritation in little, almost laughable ways. She may sigh deeply, or close the cabinets with a tad more vigor, or stamp her little body around a bit. You need the Rosetta Stone to correctly interpret her behavior.

If I can be a bit obtuse, the blame might lay with my brother. When we were growing up, he was direct with his emotions. When he smashed the television remote over my head, for example, I had no trouble comprehending his innermost feelings.

My relationship with the nurses is similar to my relationship with Ann, for better or for worse. An obvious exception is that at the hospital, I usually get to make the final decisions. I sometimes get to make the final decisions at home, too, but only when they coincide with Ann's wishes precisely. And there's also the question of numbers. It took me five years of living with Ann to realize there were moments I annoyed her. So for sixty nurses, I figure I need three centuries.

But the nurses are also the main reason I like bringing my patients to my local hospital. Both skilled and compassionate, they are the best nurses I have worked with. Enough things in life are impersonal without the most important event in a couple's life—the birth of their child—being so as well.

Traditionally, nursing is a thankless job. All I ask for is perfection. The nurses on Labor and Delivery come close. Countless times they have done the right thing, at the right time, in the right way, saving a patient from serious harm. We work closely together, under circumstances that can be stressful and sometimes painful, but are so often wonderful. So for better or for worse, it is indeed a marriage, and these nurses are people I respect, and admire, and of course, love.

But I still don't want to be awakened unnecessarily.

Despite our argument, Susie and I worked well together during the delivery, and it was a nice one. There's something so beautiful about a baby being born that makes whatever little issue is upsetting you at the moment seem trivial. By the time our patient became a mother, I wasn't mad at Susie anymore, and she wasn't mad at me—much.

Conflict with other people can be good for the soul. It teaches you about your limitations and how you can improve. I suppose with all my learning opportunities, I should be a genius by now.

It's tempting, of course, to blame other people. But assuming responsibility is usually the correct step. The only thing God has given us control over is our own actions. So I spent the drive back thinking about my late night manners.

By the time I arrived home, Ann was making breakfast. Still in a bit of denial, I indignantly told her about my hospital "reputation." Her reply was telling. "Hmmm.... I can see that."

Not getting the sympathy I craved, I went upstairs to wake my grumpy six-year-old for school. Tyler groaned when I nudged him and fought to stay asleep.

"You have the reputation of being the *worst* one in this entire family to wake up in the morning," I told him.

One eye popped open. He looked at me, perplexed. Then losing interest, he turned away and covered his head with the pillow. Tuckered out myself and tired of conflict with my fellow human beings, I crawled into bed with him and promptly fell back to sleep.

Ann jostled me awake a while later just as comfortable dreams began.

I politely expressed my gratitude.

Training Wheels

One day I left a couple in my office for a little while. When I returned, I found them laughing.

"We were just looking at your diploma," they explained.

There on the floor, leaning against the wall, was the latest addition to my office and its requisite collection of doctors' certificates: the announcement of my election to Fellowship in The American College of Obstetricians and Gynecologists. I realized it didn't mean much to most people, but to me this diploma was the culmination of the past eleven years of my life. That's ten years of formal medical training, plus one year of nagging my wife to get it framed for me.

It was such an important piece of paper that I was

stumped trying to figure out the best place to hang it. I wanted to be subtle, but I also wanted to make sure no one missed it coming into my office.

James Cross, my partner and seasoned mentor, caught me one day studying my wall space and offered a suggestion. "Why don't you just hang Christmas lights around it?"

It was a good suggestion, but not quite subtle enough. Unable to make up my mind, I let the diploma sit on the floor for a couple of weeks.

But this wasn't the diploma my patient and her husband had found so amusing. When they told me which one they liked, I realized they must have been in my office longer than I had thought. Almost hidden next to a bookcase is my very first diploma, earned in 1971. It states: "Today is a big day for you. You have finished Kindergarten, and next September you will enter first grade."

It's a piece of paper that helps keep the others in perspective. As I laughed with my patients at this anachronism, my mind served up a memory.

In kindergarten my bicycle still had training wheels. I remember moping around the garage one day after school feeling sad. My father asked me what was wrong. It's difficult for a child to put feelings into words, but my father was able to help me: it finally became clear that I was sad because my twin brother, always a little bit bigger than me, had learned to ride a two-wheeler first. With a smile, my father got out his toolbox, and off came my training wheels.

There is no better initiation into the fears and dangers of life than learning to ride a bike. How can something with two skinny tires stay up without falling? My father told me how it's done: when your bike starts to tip, turn your wheel in the direction of the fall, and you will get your balance back. My father ran alongside me the entire time. I trusted him and kept trying. I knew he would catch me before I fell.

He stayed with me hours and hours, until I could ride on my own.

I was basking in this warm memory when suddenly I realized I was daydreaming, like Homer Simpson at the nuclear power plant.

The advantage of having a wall full of diplomas is that people tend to give you the benefit of the doubt: he must be thinking about something profound and important. But my patient's husband was beginning to eye me suspiciously.

Abruptly I brought the conversation back to why they were here—ultrasound results.

A strange thing had happened. Two weeks earlier, my patient and her husband had come in for a routine visit. Our brand new, state-of-the-art, four-dimensional ultrasound machine had just arrived. It cost as much as a house. Like any male with a high-tech toy, I couldn't resist trying it out. The images were phenomenal. We could see the baby's hands and legs and face with astounding clarity. My patient was thrilled, and I was impressed at the diagnostic potentials.

But the picture revealed by the "diagnostic potentials" was unhappy. My patient had a placenta previa. Instead of attaching to the wall of the uterus, her placenta had implanted just above the cervix. This is dangerous. The path of a baby's delivery is through the cervix. The placenta is an imposing mass of blood vessels, and if it is torn during delivery, the bleeding is potentially life threatening, to both the mother and her baby.

My patient and her husband were upset. Their faces wrinkled with worry as they searched to form a question for me that might bring them hope. I offered that although the placenta completely covered her cervix, it was possible that in the coming months, as their baby grew, the placenta might rise out of the way.

Two weeks later they were back in my office, studying my diplomas, waiting for the results of a repeat ultrasound.

It was good news. Remarkably, the placenta had completely moved away from the cervix. Now it was perfectly normal. I had never seen this happen so quickly. I told them I was amazed.

My patient and her husband exchanged glances and smiled. Many people had been praying for them, they explained simply.

Prayer is viewed as a superstition by many in the medical community. The year before, I had sent a patient to a high-risk pregnancy specialist in Atlanta. His initial ultrasound had shown that her baby's legs were not growing, but a subsequent ultrasound had shown that everything was fine. This patient and her husband were certain that prayer had been the deciding factor.

But the perinatologist was dismissive: "Just an idiopathic growth delay of the baby's femurs." In other words, he didn't know, but prayer was definitely not the answer. I remember how bad this made the couple feel, that a medical authority with even more diplomas on his wall than mine would so readily discount their faith. It was as though he had taken something away from them.

Patients generously open their lives to their doctors. Sometimes we really can help. But most of the time, no matter how many diplomas hang on our walls, we are simply witnesses. We study so much science that sometimes we forget the basics, that the gift of life is just that—a miraculous gift.

My patient and her husband left my office with their prayers answered. I sat alone, looking at my kindergarten diploma and then at the new one on the floor. The last one had required an enormous effort. Becoming Board Certified was like my training wheels coming off. I was riding on my own.

There are scary moments. Despite my patients' trust, the practice of medicine is often uncertain. There is much we do not know. I am afraid to fall.

Even now that I'm an adult, it is sometimes difficult

to put feelings into words. But I understood something. Although my kindergarten diploma is perhaps the least impressive, it is the most important piece of paper on my wall. Despite our illusions of self-sufficiency, we are all children, riding a teetering, scary path through life.

My kindergarten diploma is there to remind me that even though my training wheels are off, I'll always need my Father, right alongside me, to keep me from falling.

Putting Up With Ho-Hum Miracles

A Recipe for Long Life

A Spiritual Speed Bump

The Night the Caterpillars Ate My Dinner

Sunday Morning Symphony

*"And could you keep your heart in wonder
at the daily miracles of your life,
your pain would not seem less wondrous
than your joy."*
–Kahlil Gibran

We use the word "miracle" for the wonderful, inexplicable event that defies the laws of nature. We say it is of Divine origin; we call it an act of God.

We celebrate! We like miracles. They restore our faith and remind us there is more to life than suffering and hard labors.

What we may not see is that each little moment of Life is a miracle all its own. It's not just when a baby is born. It's not just when a life is saved. It's a miracle when we awake in the morning to start a new day. And it is a miracle to love and to be loved.

We are swimming in an ocean of miracles. Moment by moment, faith reveals each one. The more clearly we see them, the more joy and health we experience each day. And the most miraculous part is this—it's all true.

A Recipe for Long Life

Our neighborhood is friendly, and there are lots of goings back and forth between our house and those of our neighbors, including, but not limited to, the mundane vacation duties one takes on when neighbors go out of town—picking up their mail, feeding the goldfish, etc. But sometimes this nice neighborliness can go a little too far.

One summer our neighbors John and Ginger were going out of town, planning to board their old black Labrador, Buck, at the vet's. My wife Ann found the timing of this hard to believe, as the dog had recently experienced a growing number of serious health problems. I was surprised he was still alive. A few months ago, he had been incontinent and could barely walk. The acupuncture sessions must really have helped.

"He's too old to be in the kennel," she explained. "He'd be hot—and lonely. Don't you think?"

I muttered an affirmative and resumed reading my paper. Saturday morning had finally arrived. It was my first day off all month and I had looked forward to spending time with my wonderful wife and children. But having just awakened, I didn't necessarily want to converse with any of them just yet.

"Then it occurred to me," Ann continued, "Buck could stay at home if someone volunteered to take care of him." My spider sense began to tingle. "So anyway, I told Ginger we'd be happy to do it."

I sagged with dread. I knew exactly what "we" meant. There's a tacit division of labor in our marriage. Barring an emergency, I wouldn't wash the sheets, just as Annie wouldn't mow the lawn. My keen husbandly instincts told me that feeding the neighbor's dog fell under my job description. But I had important tasks already on my agenda—reading the newspaper, lying on the couch, and wasting my morning away. I didn't feel like taking care of an old dog.

The clock ticked in silence. But to an experienced ear, the argument was roaring at full throttle. A few minutes later, Ann cleared her throat. Her usual smile had hardened.

"Did you say something, Honey?" I asked with as much innocence in my voice as I could muster.

"He gets fed twice a day, and he'll need an extra walk at lunchtime," she answered. "You're already late. Buck should have had breakfast an hour ago." She handed me their house key.

I stumbled down the hill to the Coopers' house, my face unshaven and my hair still a bed-headed mess. It was too close for driving, but a far enough walk so I still had time to feel sorry for myself. What was so special about Buck? I hadn't even had *my* breakfast yet. Besides, this was my weekend off.

Don't get me wrong. I love my work. It's a privilege to be entrusted with my patients' health. But it's stressful, too, particularly on Labor and Delivery, where things can change in a hurry. So I look forward to those worry-free weekends when I'm not on call.

Now, out of the blue, I was responsible for an old, sick dog—the canine equivalent of an ICU patient. What would happen to my reputation if he *died*? Unfriendly thoughts punctuated my grumbling. Why didn't they put that darn dog to sleep already? He was practically on death's door; this would have been the perfect weekend.

I unlocked the front door and entered their house. Buck was nowhere to be found. I shouted for him at the top of my lungs. No response. I called Annie, miffed she had sent me on a wild goose chase. She reassured me that indeed, this was the weekend we were to be take care of him. Then suddenly I understood—*Buck was already dead*.

Sure enough, after a ten-minute search, I found his corpse behind the couch. My medical instincts took over. How long had he been dead? If it had just happened, I would need to initiate CPR. It was the neighborly thing to do. No sooner had this occurred to me than I realized my ignorance: I must have skipped the chapter on mouth-to-dog mouth resuscitation. Half hoping rigor mortis had already set in, I nudged Buck with my foot.

He woke up.

A clinical light bulb flashed in my head. Not dead yet. Just deaf. Buck looked at me, a confused expression on his wrinkled gray face. Slowly he stood up, his bones and ligaments protesting. It hurt me just to watch. It defied logic that anything could live so long.

A note containing detailed feeding instructions was on the counter. I couldn't believe all the vitamins and medicines this dog was getting: antibiotics, digestive aids, hormone supplements, Chinese herbs—along with a vitamin enriched Kibble, *and* special canned food. Was this his secret to long life?

I reread John's instructions incredulously. Twenty pills twice a day! Just how was I going to get Buck to take all of these? My childhood experiences with our family dogs told me it wasn't possible. You'd try to disguise the medicine in a piece of food, but it never worked. Inevitably, the pill, covered with dog slobber, was gagged out on the floor. So you'd resort to the direct shove-down-the-throat-technique—one hand holding the dog's mouth shut, the other massaging his neck for a swallow reflex. It was a humiliating affair for all parties.

As I considered my options, I heard Buck drinking water in the bathroom. Sure enough, he was drinking from the toilet. Could this be his fountain of youth? I herded him back into the kitchen and pondered my next step. Even though I knew it wouldn't work, laziness prevailed, and I decided I'd just throw the pills in his dish and see what happened.

But an incredible thing occurred as I prepared his breakfast. Before my eyes, old sick Buck transformed into a frisky pup. He playfully bumped his shoulder against my leg, his eyes and mouth smiling up at me. With a gravelly woof he told me to hurry up: "I'm hungry, I'm hungry." I was intrigued. Buck's legendary appetite had made for interesting dinner conversation with John and Ginger. Once Buck had eaten two dozen fresh bagels foolishly left on the counter. Another time he had pulled open the refrigerator door with a dishtowel hanging from the handle, and had eaten a jar of mustard. During one desperate period, he'd even managed to chew open a can of soup.

By the time his breakfast was ready, Buck was wagging his tail so hard his bottom shook, and I was pretty certain he would scarf down whatever I put in his bowl. Indeed, he lunged for his dish like a wolf and finished his meal lickety-split. The pills, of course, were history. I watched bemused for several minutes, as he carefully licked the empty stainless steel bowl. That was one dish that wouldn't need cleaning. Then

Buck looked at me and licked his chops as though to say, "My compliments to the chef." He was not an old, sick dog anymore, but quite the opposite, full of life and enthusiasm.

So we had a fun weekend together, Buck and I. I fed him twice a day and walked him at lunchtime. And in return, Buck shared with me his important secret, something every physician should know–the key ingredient to living long and well. It can't be found in any medical textbook. And it's not in any vitamin, acupuncture procedure, or even water from a toilet bowl.

Buck's miraculous ingredient is joy.

A Spiritual Speed Bump

My children and my neighbors' sometimes play the modern version of "Cowboys and Indians" in my driveway, each one of the four boys armed to the teeth with a Super Soaker. A Super Soaker is the water pistol of my childhood on steroids. It looks like the best ray gun you ever imagined, and it shoots a stream of water fifty feet.

One such play day I was enjoying a book and wanted no part of their wet game. Warning glares and outright threats kept me neutral and dry for a while. But I made an irresistible target. Finally, one of them summoned the courage and let me have it, right in the face.

I dried my glasses and book, and then began the requisite interrogation. Each boy vehemently denied any responsibility. But none of them could conceal their glee. Soon they were all openly laughing with delight.

So I did what any reasonable parent would do. I grabbed the closest water gun, an Air Pressure Super Soaker XP310 (the "XP" for extra power), with one thing in mind—revenge. It was time to show these computer age Game Boy kids that even a Nintendo neophyte can keep pace. As a suburban Rambo, I quickly established that even a soaking wet boy doesn't like being squirted up the nose.

Alex, the oldest at eight, made the most challenging target. Whizzing by me on his roller blades, he gave much better than he got, laughing, screaming, and taunting all at once. Now soaking wet myself, I chased him down my driveway.

Alex was ten feet ahead, making faces at me and hurtling toward the street. Suddenly I noticed a white car speeding down my block. Horrified, I instantly became an adult. Alex was too far ahead to catch. I screamed as loud as I could for him to STOP! At the last possible moment, Alex saw the car, and in a remarkable feat of athleticism, spun himself around in a semicircle, stopping on his toes just as he passed over the curb. The white car sped by, a mere foot and a half away from his young body.

The adolescent driver never slowed or veered away.

Twelve hours later, at three o'clock in the morning, I suddenly awoke from a dead sleep. I was haunted by the image of my neighbor's son almost killed by a car. I felt guilty and stupid for chasing him. And I was angry with the reckless driver. I wondered, was this just the carelessness of an inexperienced adolescent? Or was it something more sinister—a side effect of our increasingly fast paced world, everyone in too much of a hurry to care about one another?

Awful memories flooded my mind. I remembered the twin sisters who were killed on their walk home from school. A florist's deliveryman, lost and in a hurry, reached for a map in his glove compartment and drove over the curb. Tragedy like this I saw every day as an autopsy assistant at the New York Medical Examiner's Office one summer between college semesters. Death is a diagnosis that gets the uninitiated thinking. The experience of working in a morgue taught me a lot about the fragility of life. But just like any other job, even performing autopsies became tedious after a couple of hundred had gone by. It became just another summer job.

But not for long.

One afternoon toward the end of that summer, my cousin Stephen showed up at the morgue. He had been killed a couple of blocks from his home by a girl who had just gotten her license. His face was unrecognizable. Only the name on the toe tag matched the person I remembered.

The mortician was skillful and restored Stephen's face to an almost normal appearance. But someone had to stand by the open casket to make certain he wasn't touched. His mother was so distraught she could barely stand up by herself. We gathered around her, seeking consolation for her and for ourselves. Pain and disbelief merged, enveloping us like a shroud. In the stillness that filled the spaces between the cries of anguish, the unspoken question was almost audible—where does life go?

These memories seemed as fresh as yesterday as I lay wide-awake in bed. When the telephone rang, I welcomed the distraction. A patient had arrived at the hospital in labor. The nurse sounded concerned. The baby's heart rate had been dropping. I got dressed and hurried in.

When I arrived, I saw that the readout of the baby's heart rate was indeed troubling. At another time, emergency surgery might have been brewing. But fortunately, this was my patient's third pregnancy, and the baby boy came down quickly. I placed forceps on the head and easily pulled the baby out. The umbilical cord was wrapped twice around his neck. This had been the problem. But it was easy to untangle, and in less than a minute, the baby was breathing freely and making a lot of wonderful noise. As the family surrounded its newest member, the fear and apprehension dissipated, and only hope and gratitude remained. In the stillness that sanctified the spaces between the cries of joy, another unspoken question was almost audible—where does life come from?

My ride home was more leisurely. It was still dark when I pulled into the driveway. I let out a deep sigh as I recalled the near tragedy of the day before. When we hurry unnecessarily, we don't pay attention to our path, and terrible mistakes can happen. We need reminders to slow down. So there in the early hours of the morning I wrote a letter to my neighbors, proposing a speed bump for our street.

Then I trudged upstairs and kissed the still sleeping faces of my boys and my wife, and collapsed back into bed. In places like the funeral home and the delivery room, we witness the mysterious comings and goings of life. And in those places, in the presence of birth and death, we no longer hurry as we approach the stillness of the Eternal. Like spiritual speed bumps, these moments compel us to slow down and to see what is right before us—God's fragile gift of life.

I thought about my neighbor's near accident and I recognized it as a spiritual speed bump. A warm spring of gratitude welled up inside me for what, this time, was only the gentlest of reminders.

The Night the Caterpillars Ate My Dinner

Many years have passed since the night I delivered my first baby and, in retrospect, it is clear that practicing obstetrics was the path the Creator intended me to take. But I confess that after a thousand deliveries, the blaze of emotions that once accompanied each one has subsided to a softer glow, flaring up again only at those times when danger, or joy, bring the world more sharply into focus.

So it was with a recent difficult birth. The mother and her family were well known to me. Two years earlier I had delivered my patient's second daughter. Her first daughter, then an irrepressible nine-year-old, had gleefully cut the cord. But with this labor, the third daughter, there were complications. The baby's heart rate kept falling.

It was obvious to my patient that I was worried. Every five minutes I came into the room, obsessing over the baby's heart rate like an anxious stockbroker watching the ticker tape. I maintained a professional demeanor with my patient, trying to give her as much reassurance as I could. Her anxiety level was rising and, for a moment, I felt bad. When confronted with worrisome clinical circumstances, doctors tend to pull back emotionally. It helps us think clearly and, hopefully, make the right decisions.

It's a mistake to think that any physician knows exactly what he or she is doing at all times, and, at this moment, I was no exception. I was uncertain about what was wrong. But finally a routine procedure improved the baby's heart rate, averting emergency surgery. The baby was born. My patient's first daughter, now eleven, delightedly cut her second cord. Her little sister's cry filled the room. My tension dissipated. I was a third year medical student discovering my destiny once again, and my soul hummed with the joy that swelled the room.

When I arrived home that evening, my stomach was also humming—with hunger. I looked forward to a nourishing meal and sharing the stories of my day.

My wife, Ann, is my soul mate. Well, she's either my soul mate or just a very good listener. It doesn't matter. Ann is a loving person, a supportive friend, a great mother to our children and, most importantly, an attentive audience. So even though she's heard me talk about clinical cases hundreds of times, I knew she'd listen to me with polite fascination.

And, she would feed me.

But this night I was wrong. When I walked in the door my first clue was that supper was nowhere to be seen. My second was that Ann expressed no interest in the heroics of my day. Instead, she wanted to tell me all about *her* day.

It was an outrage.

Incredibly, Ann and the boys were actually ignoring me. They were engrossed in a large glass jar on the kitchen counter which contained, upon inspection, caterpillars. I groaned under my breath—the evening's conversation was going to revolve around Ann's butterfly garden, again. She shot me a dark look. My groan had apparently been less discreet than I intended. I gave myself a mental kick. Now I'd have to work even harder to feign interest.

Last year, after months of research—otherwise known as shopping from gardening catalogs—Ann created a butterfly garden in our backyard. She told me all about it but the details escape me—something about attracting lots of bugs to our yard.

In its execution, the project fell short of Ann's expectations. Deer and rabbits showed their enthusiasm by chowing down on her plants. In the end, Ann counted a grand total of five butterflies the entire summer. She was depressed. So was

I. All the plants she'd ordered had been a waste of money, and now I had to console her about it, to boot.

Then, one morning, Ann returned from a visit to her garden practically skipping. Two monarch caterpillars were eating her milkweed plants. Several times a day, Ann took our two sons out to watch the bugs. After a few days, according to their frequent and detailed bulletins, the caterpillars had eaten *all* the milkweed.

So, I came home this particular evening in a good mood after a delivery to find that Ann and the boys had spent two hours gathering food for the caterpillars. The air went out of my balloon. Ann enthusiastically badgered me into pressing my ear against the jar so I could hear the caterpillars munching on the milkweed leaf dinners she and the boys had so thoughtfully and painstakingly prepared.

I took the subtle approach:

"They sound really hungry. I know how they must feel.

"Boy, it must be nice to eat your fill.

"You've done a really nice job fixing dinner—for the caterpillars."

I tried to be a good sport. I'd heard that Monarch butterflies are endangered. Freezes in Mexico and genetically-engineered corn with poison pollen are said to be wiping them out. These are the facts you pick up when your wife has a butterfly garden. I proudly recited my extensive knowledge about Monarchs in an effort to show Ann that, in fact, I *was* listening to her all those months. But she informed me, to my surprise, that Monarchs may not be so endangered after all, just underestimated by butterfly experts.

That was the final straw! A couple of bugs not even on the endangered species list were keeping me from my dinner. But Ann was so enchanted, she didn't notice how annoyed I was. I adopted the guise of supportive husband and took the family out to the local pizza parlor. The caterpillars came along for the ride. My mouth was watering by the time the cheese breadsticks arrived. Joseph, our five-year-old, launched into a rambling grace, thanking God for the cater-pillars who had come to our yard ... who were going to grow into orange butterflies ... and fly away into the sky ....

As I half-listened to his thankful litany, my mind wan-dered back to the delivery. I gave silent thanks for my patient's healthy baby. I remembered her ultrasound: the tiny fetus, much smaller than a caterpillar, now a beautiful baby girl living and breathing in the world. Metamorphosis is the way of life. We grow, we become, and ultimately our souls soar skyward, like the Monarch.

I stared at Ann and the boys, their eyes closed as Joseph was reaching his grand finale. Tyler frowned with impa-tience. I laughed to myself. Sometimes the beauty of life is so intense, it overwhelms us with its light. At these moments, the path before you is clearly illuminated, and faith becomes effortless.

Before taking my first bite of dinner, it occurred to me that these are the moments, and nothing more, for which we truly hunger.

Sunday Morning Symphony

Our good friends Jamie and Tracey Whitehouse often come to visit for long weekends. A few years ago, on one particular visit, our alarm clock was their eighteen-month-old son, serenading us with his screams each morning before first light. For three days in a row, this little rooster unfailingly woke the entire house.

One of my favorite quotations is by Benjamin Franklin, and it usually comes to mind only when my in-laws visit. "Guests are like fish: after three days, they both begin to stink." On that Sunday morning, in addition to the screams of the child, the house filled with the aroma of a dirty diaper.

My grumpy mood quickly deteriorated into an argument with Ann.

During an argument, I usually experience only two emotions—anger, and then more anger. But this time I also felt confusion. Why were we arguing on such a beautiful Sunday? Ann and Tracey were stressed out, and our beautiful children sounded like urchins in a street fight, but otherwise it was a perfect autumn morning to spend with people you love.

I tried to retreat into my pre-church Sunday morning routine with my three best friends—the newspaper, the couch, and the coffee pot. But I couldn't find the newspaper. My coffee got knocked over by one of the beautiful children, and my brand new couch now bore a wet coffee stain.

Ann herded the children into the basement before Dad blew a vessel. She insisted that they first clean up their toys. They resisted. Now Ann was angry, too.

That may not have been the best time to ask her to get me a replacement cup of coffee.

Ann was nineteen when we first met. She was happy all of the time. As our relationship flowered, I noticed that she had some occasional sad moments. After we were married and living together, the sad moments came more often, and there came a few angry moments as well. After we had two children, the range of her emotions came into full display.

It's almost as though having a husband and children to deal with had something to do with it.

Now, in front of our friends on this flawed Sunday morning, Ann and I argued unselfconsciously about nothing. For a moment I forgot about all the wonderful things Ann does for me and remembered all the things she failed to do. Typical male thinking, I believe. Or perhaps, typical male lack of thinking.

In my medical experience, I have found that there is really only one cure for this kind of family discord—a box of fresh donuts.

So I gathered up the boys into the minivan, and off we went to the local bakery.

Like all children, ours are the owners of beautiful souls immortal—camouflaged by poorly developed social skills. The problem is that children have minds of their own. Tell them what to do, and they tell you what they want to do. We don't want mindless little automatons, blindly obeying our every command. But once in a while, it wouldn't be so bad.

On the way to the bakery, Tyler and Joseph were in top form, laughing, whining, arguing. We went through all the knock-knock jokes, and then sang the alphabet. Tyler's rendition surprised me, and I told him he forgot the "p." "No I didn't, Dad," he said, "It's down your leg!" Tyler calls me Dad now, not Daddy. How come? I ask him. "Daddy" is embarrassing, he tells me. But he will be happy, he adds, to call me "Doody."

Outside the bakery, our Three Stooges routine was interrupted by an odd sound. The big, glass-vaulted entrance was filled with the chirping of birds. We looked up and saw them swooping through the air, fluttering back and forth, singing their hearts out. The boys bugged me to go get the donuts, but I was mesmerized. The sight and sound of that Sunday morning symphony of bird song was an unmistakable affirmation from the Creator. I wondered why this beautiful music—why here, why now?

It was a typical outing with the boys: "Don't touch the donuts Tyler. Don't cough on the donuts Joseph…."

On our way out we paused at the entrance to listen to the birds some more. But they had quieted down, perching and preening in the rafters.

When we got home with our peace offering of donuts, Ann and I hugged and apologized. The children returned to the basement playroom and we adults sat quietly upstairs, drinking our coffee, reading the paper. I thought about the avian symphony—God's music. Had I witnessed only a bird family argument? The music was beautiful, nonetheless. Maybe our family arguments were just a part of God's music, too—part of the wonderful, complicated, human symphony He has created from our lives.

It would take another thirty minutes for me to fully shake my grumpy mood. But I realized that, despite the occasional arguments and chaos of raising children, these are wonderful times, perhaps the best they'll ever be. And I felt an emotion grow inside me, an emotion that led to a smile.

I Don't Believe – I Know

– My Children Will Have Faith –

– The Room for Tough Questions –

– Healing: Giving Credit Where It Is Due –

– A Long Walk –

While Jesus was still speaking, some men came from the house of Jairus, the synagogue ruler.

"Your daughter is dead," they said. "Why bother the teacher anymore?"

Ignoring what they said, Jesus told the synagogue ruler, "Don't be afraid; just believe."

When they came to the home of the synagogue ruler, Jesus saw a commotion, with people crying and wailing loudly.

He went in and said to them, "Why all this commotion and wailing? The child is not dead but asleep."

But they laughed at him.

After he put them all out ... he took her by the hand and said to her, "Little girl, I say to you, get up!"

Immediately the girl stood up and walked around.

–Mark 5:35-42

*"What do you want me to do for you?"
Jesus asked him.*

*The blind man said, "Rabbi, I want to
see."*

*"Go," said Jesus, "your faith has healed
you."*

*Immediately he received his sight and
followed Jesus along the road.*

—Mark 10:51-52

The 20th century psychologist Carl Jung believed that spiritual experience was essential to our well-being. When asked during a 1959 BBC interview if he believed in the existence of God, Jung replied, "I don't believe. I know."

Faith is a form of knowingness. Its power pierces the veil of contemporary skepticism. With the clear sight that faith provides, we perceive that there is much in life that cannot be explained by a model as limited as science. Those who rely upon its achievements are still waiting to glimpse what those with faith have already seen. Faith conveys knowledge that science has yet to reveal.

As a physician, I am drawn to the role of Jesus as Healer. Stories of his life describe acts of healing that modern medicine cannot explain. Two thousand years later, from my patients and friends, have come miracle stories, too—miracles in which the power of the Eternal Healer is so evident that it defies the childlike insistence of the unbeliever. God has bestowed upon us a mystery in this gift of life. When we attempt to understand its nature, faith in His presence illuminates our perceptions in a way that a scientific perspective does not. Faith deepens our understanding of life and in fact, forms the basis of health itself. Jesus spoke a universal truth in His utterance, "Your faith has healed you."

Cast off the anchor of skepticism. Sail with the wind of faith. You might discover on your voyage that the Kingdom of Heaven is truly all around you.

My Children Will Have Faith

A single surgical clamp, placed on the bleeding vessels of a ruptured fallopian tube, can save a patient's life.

I know this because I have placed these clamps myself. Ten years ago, a patient arrived at the emergency room of Grady Hospital in shock from such a rupture and the resulting loss of blood. I was a fourth year Chief Resident on call for the surgical emergency. After placing the clamp, I instructed my pretty, wide-eyed junior resident to suction the half gallon of blood and clots from the patient's abdomen and pelvis. I remember keeping my voice calm, to emphasize the achievement of total control—"Just another day in the operating room, ma'am."

I tried to limit my swagger as we walked to the waiting

room to reassure the patient's family and give them the good news. But afterward, alone in the call room in my blood-stained scrubs, I allowed myself to bask in the full power of my accumulated years of study and training. I felt a Cheshire cat smile of self-congratulation steal over my face.

Always a mistake.

A superb textbook on obstetrics and gynecology opens with Alexander Pope's famous refrain,

> "A little learning is a dang'rous thing;
> Drink deep, or taste not the Pierian Spring;
> There shallow draughts intoxicate the brain,
> And drinking largely sobers us again."

Many times I had flipped to re-read that quote before diving into my studies. It was a warning to the overconfident. But on that day toward the end of my eighth year of training, I fell into the deep sleep of the self-satisfied. At last, I knew exactly what I was doing and what was going on in the world.

A phone call the next day proved how wrong I was.

The caller was Ife Sofola. Ife (pronounced Ee-fay) was one of my classmates from medical school. A tall, muscular Nigerian, Ife was not only a brilliant student, but a man of deep compassion and undeniable charisma. His easy smile, booming laugh, and lilting Nigerian accent were a comfort and delight to both friends and patients. At the time, he was a flight surgeon at the renowned Bethesda Naval Hospital, where our Presidents receive their medical care.

Ife had called to let me know that his mother had died. But it wasn't the sorrow he wanted to share. It was the miracle.

Months earlier, Ife's family learned that his mother was dying from liver failure. Brought to the Bethesda Naval Hospital, she fell into a coma. She was put under a DNR order—Do Not Resuscitate. Those orders are reserved for patients who cannot be saved. The words are a kind of final acknowledgement: that modern medicine has failed the patient, that we can do nothing, that Death is coming.

But Ife and his siblings were not ready to let go of their mother. They had been already heartsick with the loss of their father, who had died earlier that year. The looming loss of their mother was too much to bear.

Desperate to do something, Ife's sister sought out a friend of a friend of a friend who was reputed to be a "healer"—someone who could save life where others had failed. Ife's sister flew the healer to America from Nigeria, keeping it a secret from her family until the healer showed up at Bethesda. A student of medical science, Ife was dismayed and agitated by his arrival. But there was nothing to lose, so he and his siblings permitted the healer to stay.

The healer directed them to hold hands around the

dying woman's bed. They prayed in silence for five minutes. Then the healer announced, "It is done." With that he departed, taking a taxi back to the airport.

Twenty minutes later, Ife's mother awoke. She smiled and greeted her family and got out of bed to take a shower. Ife said there were no words to describe how dumbstruck her physicians were. Ife himself, exuberant, believing, brimming with unadulterated joy, raced and leaped down the hallways in his white coat, yelling so all could hear, "A miracle has occurred! Here, at Bethesda! A MIRACLE!"

Within a few weeks, Ife's mother succumbed to her disease and died. But not before she had left the hospital and spent precious days with her children at home saying goodbye. Her explanation of what had happened was simple and profound. "I came back," she said to her children, "so you would have faith."

The power of modern medicine is an illusion. The physician's sense of mastery, the gratitude of patients and their families—all these constitute a thin veneer which sometimes covers the truth. The source of the healing lies far beyond our earthly skills. It emanates from the realm of the Unknowable—from God, the Source of Life.

The other day a patient told me she was confident about her upcoming surgery, "because I have faith in you." A decade ago I would have enjoyed that kind of comment. The trust and respect of patients is a blessing. But the truth is that we are all participants—patients and physicians alike—holding hands in a circle of healing and praying for a miracle. And we are blessed with this miracle of healing every day we live.

Ife concluded his call to me with his own revelation. His tone was not one of grief, but excitement.

"Michael," Ife said to me, his voice trembling, "how many hours did we spend in the lecture hall? How many books did we read? How many operations have we performed? We think we are doctors, so we must know something about life and death." He paused for a long moment. "I tell you this, Michael—we know nothing. Nothing."

I fumbled for words. I said his story was just amazing, that it had changed my life.

Ife laughed his large, unforgettable laugh. "And well it should, Michael—well it should."

The Room for Tough Questions

I plopped down in a chair outside the Intensive Care Unit and took a deep breath. It was a busy night, even for Grady, and I was starting to feel overwhelmed. We had just completed back-to-back surgeries, and a third patient was on her way to the operating room.

The sound of a dry hacking cough from the ICU refocused my thoughts. It was Miss Roberts. I had come to check on her before the next surgery. I grabbed her chart and looked at her vitals. Her grandmother had called an ambulance for her twelve hours ago when she had trouble breathing. The diagnosis was viral pneumonia. Miss Roberts was pregnant, and this made the pneumonia especially dangerous. Only fifteen years old, she had kept her pregnancy secret the entire seven months.

"She's not sounding too good, Delia," I said. "How's she doing?"

Delia, Miss Robert's nurse, had worked in the Grady ICU for more years than I had been alive. So her opinion was important. But we weren't exactly best friends, and her scowl deepened at the sound of my voice. Leafing through her magazine, she had ignored me when I sat down. To her I was just another young white doctor passing through, and I'd be gone before long. But I was a Chief Resident now, not a frightened, green intern, so finally she deigned to answer.

"Nope. She be sounding worse and worse." Delia glanced up at the fetal monitor. "Baby still okay tho'... for now."

Even from the nurse's station, I could hear Miss Roberts' labored breathing. She was getting tired. How long before she was so exhausted she could no longer breathe? I could picture the scene—a STAT call on the overhead speakers, the code team converging on the ICU, chest compressions, ventilation, and, of course, the unborn baby's heart rate crashing right along with its mother's. Miss Roberts was young and strong, and once hooked to a ventilator, she'd probably be okay. But what would happen to her unborn baby? Brain damage? Death?

What bothered me most was that this impending emergency was preventable. We needed to put Miss Roberts on the ventilator now, before she stopped breathing. We could let the machine breathe for her so she could rest and recover from the infection. The problem was Grandma Roberts—she refused to give permission. She was the child's guardian. Without her consent our hands were tied. I had been warned about Grandma Roberts when I came on duty. "Stay away from her, Mike. She's difficult. She's irrational. And she'll bite your head off."

But I can be difficult and irrational myself. This gave me unique insight. Besides, it's better to prevent an emergency than to respond to one. I was certain I could change her mind.

But she bit off my head as easily as a kid attacks a gingerbread cookie. After ten minutes, I had had enough. I documented her refusal just as my colleague had and decided the best strategy was avoidance.

I placed my stethoscope on Miss Robert's back. Her lungs sounded as bad as her chest X-ray looked. But she and her baby were holding on, so I decided to start my other surgery. It was almost visiting hour, and I wasn't in the mood for another dressing down by Grandma Roberts.

I almost got away.

"You wait right there," an angry voice called out. My back stiffened. I slowly turned around.

"What you doin' for my grandbaby?" Grandma Roberts asked, her finger aimed at my throat like a knife. She didn't like my explanation. Still. "Her momma went on a machine just like that one and she was dead and in the ground in two weeks' time. I ain't letting you know-nothin' doctah's put no tube down her throat!"

My mind wandered—if I could put a tube down Grandma's throat, I wouldn't have to listen to her anymore.

But I understood her position. Five years earlier, her cocaine-addicted daughter, Miss Roberts' mother, had been placed on a ventilator when she was dying from AIDS. The terminal nature of her disease had made that an entirely different situation, of course. But Grandma Roberts was filled with a fear that kept her from hearing me, no matter what I said. Since I couldn't guarantee her granddaughter would be fine, she decided I didn't know what I was doing. She insisted on speaking with someone who "got the answers."

Delia didn't say a word as she listened to me fend off Grandma Robert's accusations. But her ever-present scowl began to soften. She was enjoying the abuse I was receiving—until suddenly, she became the target.

"... and all you do behind the counter is sit your ugly butt down and read your paper!" Grandma Roberts turned on Delia, pointing her accusatory finger. "You lazy and don't care 'bout my grandbaby. No one 'round here care...."

This was a welcome change. But attacking an old Grady nurse like Delia is like poking a sleeping grizzly with a stick.

"What you say to me?" Delia shouted. She threw her

magazine down and stood up. "You the one who don't care nothin'! Your grandbaby real sick and you won't let us do what we s'posed to do!"

The argument took off like a rocket. I would have enjoyed watching the entire fifteen rounds, but this was my chance to escape. I almost got away again, but just before I entered the OR, Delia took an illegal blow. She STAT paged Grady Security to the ICU.

I'd witnessed emotionally distraught family members dragged away from patient care areas by Security. Rarely necessary, it made sad situations sadder. So I ran back to the ICU where I found them still screaming at each other. Cautiously I entered the fray. Struck with an inspiration, I pulled Grandma Roberts to the side and whispered in her ear.

"Do you want to talk to someone who has all the answers? Someone who can promise you your grandbaby is going to be OK?"

Grandma Roberts glowered at me. "That's what I been sayin'... ."

"Room 143A—there's someone waiting for you right now." She looked at me with a raised eyebrow. I gave her my word, pointing the way. Delia was infuriated when she realized I was letting Grandma Roberts go.

What a relief it was to leave the chaos behind and enter the blessed sanctuary of the operating room. Life can be so confusing and frightening. How comforting it is to focus on one thing, and forget about everything else. The surgery went well and was over far too soon. Reluctantly, I walked back to the ICU. My jaw dropped in surprise at the scene that greeted me.

Grandma Roberts was sitting at the nurses' station weeping uncontrollably, and Delia was hugging on her like they were long lost sisters. My first thought was that Miss Roberts had died. I checked the monitors. She and baby were fine.

Grandma Roberts saw me. "Dr. Litrel. I 'pologize for my rude behavior b'fuh," she said between sobs. "I 'preciate all you doin' for my grandbaby. I'm just so scared. You were right—Room 143A. I got my answers, I got my answers. You put my grandbaby on that breathin' machine."

Within twenty minutes, Miss Roberts was on the ventilator. Her body was now able to rest. She came off the ventilator in two days, and within a week, was healthy enough to go home.

Hidden, unexpectedly, in a dark corner of the enormous thousand-bed inner city hospital is an important room hardly used enough, Room 143A. It's a chapel, tiled in marble, with old wooden pews—a place where the most difficult questions are sometimes most eloquently answered.

Healing: Giving Credit Where It Is Due

The young mother-to-be was already in the operating room when I arrived at the hospital. Minutes earlier the nurses had called me in. The patient had been in the elevator headed for labor and delivery when her water had suddenly ruptured. The umbilical cord—the lifeline between the baby and the mother—had fallen out. It was a surgical emergency.

The patient hadn't seen a doctor her entire pregnancy. When I came in she was screaming and writhing on the narrow operating room table. Her cervix wasn't completely opened, so her baby couldn't simply be pulled out. A crash cesarean was the only option. I looked over at the anesthesiologist. No time to put on scrubs: he was in his street clothes, and so was I. He put the patient to sleep the fast way as the nurses splashed on some Betadine antiseptic and covered her with drapes. I made the incision, a foot long, straight down from her belly button.

The baby was out in twenty seconds. But he was unconscious, with no apparent pulse. The pediatrician began CPR while I brought the mother's bleeding under control. Rapid action and shouts had filled the operating room before the delivery. But now, as we caught our breath and finished the job, there was only silence. My hands were shaking from the adrenaline. Had we been fast enough?

A minute later, a faint cry provided the answer. "You can do it, baby!" the pediatrician exhorted. As the cry got steadily louder, happiness spread contagiously among us, and the operating room was soon abuzz with excited voices. This had been a close one. It was after midnight when we finished. Cookies and juice at the nurse's station made for an impromptu party as we celebrated our success before going home. In retrospect, with a healthy mother in the recovery room and a crying baby in the nursery, the delivery had been a lot of fun.

It had been stressful, too, but that's just part of the job. And besides, it wasn't nearly as stressful as what was on my agenda the next evening—shopping for groceries with my children.

In the operating room you have the illusion of control. There is only one task, one for which you have trained extensively, and a half dozen skilled people are gathered around, dedicated to helping you accomplish this task. But in the grocery store, alone with your children, you suddenly realize there is no possible training to prepare you for this. And no one is coming to help you.

Can we get this, Daddy? Why not, Daddy? Please, please, Daddy! But I want it, Daddy. I don't like you, Daddy. How about this? How about that?

I was hoarse from yelling and we hadn't even made it out of the produce aisle. There we were, Kroger's own private demolition team, me with the grocery cart navigating unfamiliar terrain, my boys running up and down the aisles, grabbing things off the shelves, knocking things down, arguing, whining, crying. I was about to lose it, along with the remainder of my hair.

In the midst of the chaos I was hailed by someone. It took a moment to place her, and then I felt embarrassed. She was a former surgery patient. It's perfectly acceptable for friends and family to witness my parental struggles. But I try to maintain a semblance of professionalism in the presence of patients.

My patient regarded me with bemusement.

She had recovered well from her hysterectomy and bladder surgery, she told me, no longer experiencing any pain or leakage. I was, as always, gratified. But her appreciation continued until it crossed the boundary into the profuse—an awkward moment. As a surgical mentor used to say, "People get better despite what we do, not because of what we do." I was not responsible for her healing. I was more a witness to it than anything else, and I told her as much.

My patient nodded as though she understood *exactly* what I meant—and then she shared a remarkable story. A dozen years earlier, her two-year-old had been hospitalized for a life threatening infection. Her daughter was so dehydrated she couldn't lift her head without assistance. My patient, distraught and frightened, never left her daughter's bedside. Late one night in her vigil, as my patient rummaged through her daughter's diaper bag, a book fell out. It was a book about faith written by Norman Vincent Peale. A friend had given it to her. My patient had always been scientifically minded, and gave little credence to notions like faith or prayer. But, desperate to try anything that might bring about her daughter's well being, she decided to give it a spin.

Fearful of embarrassment should someone see her, she closed the door before kneeling next to her child's crib. She prayed, "Dear God, if you are real, please heal my child." As she touched her daughter's face, she felt a jolt of energy rush through her daughter's body. The little girl, who had been unable to even lift her head, awoke as though it were morning and began to crawl around her crib. Within hours her improvement was dramatic and undeniable, and in a few days, she left the hospital.

Practitioners of modern medicine are sometimes guilty of the comfortable belief that they have everything under control. Technology, pharmaceuticals, and surgery provide a great arsenal against disease and suffering. But let's be honest—we don't really *understand* what's going on. No medical library holds the answer to the question, why do we heal?

All medical therapies have risks. But no matter what assistance is provided, the gift of healing is never less than a miracle. One ancient form of therapy is still practiced by those with faith. The therapy, often discounted by the scientific, carries no risks, and sometimes, surprising benefits.

Prayer.

A Long Walk

My wife Ann once asked me what was wrong with the hinges on the kitchen cabinets. After a sober, manly inspection, I assured her they were fine. Then why, she asked in an innocent voice, do they never close after you open them?

I was on to her one day when she asked if the lenses on my glasses were scratched. I feigned deafness and hid behind my newspaper. The fire was crackling, the Christmas tree lights were twinkling, and the couch was soft. It was the perfect way to recover from a long night's work at the hospital. I wasn't in the mood for a dissection of my personal shortcomings, no matter how fascinating the conversation might become. But the newspaper couldn't save me. I learned that I do not put my dirty clothing *inside* the laundry basket.

Ann was curious to know if I believed my clothing magically made its way from the floor into the laundry basket. Or did I grasp that another human being was somehow involved in the process?

I defended myself with a rhetorical question. Am I jeopardizing someone's life by leaving my dirty clothing on the floor? This is a neat doctor trick I learned way back in medical school. Pay close attention to the subtleties. I am reminding my wife that in my profession, life and death decisions are sometimes made. This makes what I do seem important. Simultaneously—and this is the fun part—I am also belittling what Ann does.

My thinly-veiled point was that it should be an honor for her to pick up my dirty laundry, so shut up and leave me alone.

But Ann was exhausted, too. The children had been fighting all afternoon. She had barely made a dent in her day's work. And her husband, instead of lending a hand when he came home, had crashed on the couch. Now that same husband—a bona fide expert in women's health and well versed in the difficulties of womanhood—was trivializing her role in our family as both a mother and a wife. My neat doctor trick exploded in my face.

An argument ensued.

Having worked throughout the previous night with little sleep I had looked forward to resting in the bosom of my family. What I found were yelling kids in the background and a nagging wife in the foreground. I couldn't decide if I wanted to scream or cry or just break an expensive glass object.

Instead, I opted for a long walk.

An oath I took seventeen years ago included the promise "for better or for worse." Blessed with beautiful children, a beautiful wife, and good health, I understood intellectually, as upset as I was, that this still fell under the "for better" category. But it sure as heck felt like "for worse." Why is it that the people you love the most are also the most annoying?

The chilly night air took some of the heat from my anger and my thoughts drifted back to a long walk I took many years ago. I was staying with my parents in New York during the Christmas break between semesters my sophomore year in college. I awoke in the middle of the night, restless and troubled. For a long while I sat by my parents' Christmas tree trying to sort it out. Then I drove to Jones Beach on Long Island's South Shore and began walking.

A young woman I hardly knew was critically ill. She was an artist, a student at the University of Michigan, whom I'd met just two months earlier on a visit with my brother. I was attending college in Connecticut, but she and I had stayed in touch by phone. I had called her the day before at her parents' home in Valdosta, Georgia, and was shocked to discover she was in the intensive care unit at Emory University. Her brain had started to bleed from a birth defect she never knew she had. There was a significant chance she would die.

I walked for miles on that empty winter beach. Waves crashed unseen in darkness, the wind blew cold. The night sky glittered with stars. Life can appear futile sometimes. Why do we suffer? Why do we die? As a student of science, I had learned that life on Earth emerged from the ocean billions of years ago. Our sun is but one star in an ocean of stars which number like grains of sand on a beach. What do one person's concerns matter when compared to the infinity of the universe? I thought about my friend and felt helpless. The scientist in me had always viewed faith in God as a crutch for people who were afraid to die. I felt truly alone.

The pain of my loneliness overwhelmed me. So, on that cold December night, I opened my heart to God for the first time, I think, and prayed in earnest.

God answered. I heard no deep booming voice from the sky, but instead I felt a new understanding that seemed to nourish my soul—*Life is My gift to each of you, every moment priceless. Treasure this gift, no matter the pain, trust in Me, let go of your worries, let go of your pain.*

I felt comforted as I had never been before. I still worried whether my art student friend would survive. But I knew for certain that I was not alone, nor was she, and that none of us ever are. She might die. I would mourn her death then, but I would do so with faith in God's hand on our lives. Tomorrow had not been promised to any of us. God's gift of life was to be celebrated today.

Recalling that long walk and the understanding it opened in my heart reminded me that an argument with my wife was no way to celebrate this gift. When I got home, I apologized. It wasn't the first time we had gotten into a stupid fight, and wouldn't be the last. I had been gone long enough that Ann had time to cool down, too, and she'd even started worrying about me.

We relaxed together as a family by the Christmas tree just before the boys' bedtime. Ann and I were still a little annoyed with each other. But we laughed as we made up. I assured her that I didn't think it was a privilege for her to clean up after me. She confessed that she knew my glasses weren't scratched. And after awhile, as I sat with my family, I understood that this was one of the happiest moments of my life.

The neurosurgeon who treated my art student friend all those years ago declared that she made a complete recovery from her bleed. But she and I still laugh and wonder aloud if she might have suffered just a little brain damage in one respect—when she agreed to marry me.